MARCO  POLO

FLOR ENCE

GERMANY
SWITZERLAND AUSTRIA
ITALY SLOVENIA
FRANCE CROATIA
○Genoa
MC Florence BOSNIA-
○ RSM HERZEG
Corsica
(F)
○Rome
○ Naples
Sardinia Ischia
Mediterranean Sea

T0150574

FREE!

THE
TOURING APP

shows you the way...
including routes and offline maps!

GET MORE OUT OF YOUR MARCO POLO GUIDE

IT'S AS SIMPLE AS THIS

1 go.marco-polo.com/flo

2 download and discover

GO!

WORKS OFFLINE!

SYMBOLS

INSIDER TIP	Insider Tip
★	Highlight
🔵🔵🔵⚫	Best of...
☼	Scenic view
🌍	Responsible travel: for eco-logical or fair trade aspects
(*)	Telephone numbers that are not toll-free

**PRICE CATEGORIES
HOTELS**

Expensive	over 170 euros
Moderate	100–170 euros
Budget	under 100 euros

Prices are for a double room
per night, breakfast usually
included

**PRICE CATEGORIES
RESTAURANTS**

Expensive	over 30 euros
Moderate	15–30 euros
Budget	under 15 euros

Prices are for a typical complete meal in the particular
restaurant

On the cover: Visit David at the Galleria dell'Accademia p. 41 | Everyone meets at the Rivoire p. 64

MAPS IN THE GUIDEBOOK
(130 A1) Page numbers and coordinates refer to the street atlas and the map of Florence and surrounding area on p. 140/141

Coordinates are also given for places that are not marked on the street atlas.
(0) Site/address located off the map

(*A–B 2–3*) refers to the removable pull-out map

INSIDE FRONT COVER:
The best Highlights

INSIDE BACK COVER:
Plan of the public transport network

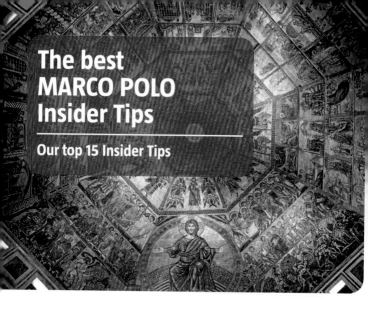

The best MARCO POLO Insider Tips

Our top 15 Insider Tips

INSIDER TIP ▶ Dazzling mosaics
The golden glow of the Byzantine mosaics in the octagonal *Battistero di San Giovanni* is second to none in Florence (photo above) → p. 29

INSIDER TIP ▶ Truffle rolls and prosecco
See and be seen: elegant Florentines have taken their aperitif at *Procacci* since 1885, along with the famous *panino tartufato* → p. 65

INSIDER TIP ▶ Dining and theatre
The former salt store transforms itself each evening into an extraordinary restaurant with a varied show: *Teatro del Sale* → p. 86

INSIDER TIP ▶ Balcony high above the city
From the *Forte di Belvedere* you have a picture-perfect view over Florence to the hilltops of Fiesole in the distance – a truly unforgettable experience if an open-air exhibition is currently showing! → p. 54

INSIDER TIP ▶ Essence of Italy
Mix with regulars at the *Gozzi Sergio* trattoria who come here in appreciation of the traditional and home-cooked Tuscan cuisine → p. 71

INSIDER TIP ▶ Balmy nights in Fiesole
Florentine summer nights at a ballet performance of the *Estate Fiesolana* under the starry skies at the Teatro Romano in Fiesole are unforgettable → p. 108

INSIDER TIP ▶ City hotel with car park
In Florence, a rarity: driving your car in the garden of the city-centre hotel *Royal* and leaving it there → p. 95

INSIDER TIP ▶ Rose water
They've been distilling the delicate *acqua di rose* at the *Officina Profumo Farmaceutica di Santa Maria Novella,* part of the former monastery, since 1381 → p. 77

INSIDER TIP Horses in church

In the deconsecrated Romanesque San Pancrazio Church, you can visit the horse sculptures of Marino Marini as well as the *Sacello Rucellai* which was bricked until recently → p. 47

INSIDER TIP Artisans in the princess's garden

The *Artigianato e Palazzo* (photo below) exhibition is extremely popular with Florence's high society who come to buy the finest Italian craftsmanship. Don't miss out! → p. 114

INSIDER TIP Lunch with Dante

Lunch-time menu for just 16 euros at one of the best and (in the evening) most expensive restaurants in the city: *Alle Murate* → p. 66

INSIDER TIP A space for modern art – at last

A breath of fresh air in the *Museo Novecento* for Italian 20th century masterpieces → p. 47

INSIDER TIP Picture-book cinema

A visit to the *Odeon Cinehall* has an air of Hollywood about it. You sit in deep, plush seats, in the middle of this genuine 1920s cinema theatre. During the week, films are shown in the original English daily → p. 86

INSIDER TIP Lunch at the market hall

If you want to eat well, but fast, as well as fresh and regionally, feast at the stalls on the newly designed top floor of the *Mercato Centrale* → p. 71

INSIDER TIP A market of yore

Tourists seldom make it out to the *Mercato di Sant'Ambrogio*. The stalls of the fruit and vegetable sellers are grouped outside around this fine cast-iron market hall from 1873 with all its little shops. People buy, sell, haggle and talk, which is no wonder, since everybody has known each other for years → p. 80

BEST OF...

GREAT PLACES FOR FREE
Discover new places and save money

FOR FREE

● *Art on Sundays*

If you happen to be in the city on the first Sunday in the month, you'll be lucky enough to catch *DomenicalMuseo* when all the state museums offer free admission – from the Uffizi Gallery and Medici Chapels to the Galleria dell'Accademia with Michelangelo's David (photo) → p. 33

● *City tour with bus No C3*

The *electric minibus C3* drives through the narrow streets of old Florence, past the Piazza Pitti and Piazza Santa Croce and crosses the Arno several times. This makes it the cheapest city tour – not completely free of course, but for a mere 1.20 euros → p. 123

● *A break at the library*

You can sit virtually undisturbed under the arcades of the cloisters at the *Biblioteca delle Oblate*. Brunelleschi's dome is so close you could almost touch it, and there's a play area for the kids. The setting costs nothing, so you can treat yourself to a cappuccino and a brioche → p. 50

● *Open air sculpture gallery*

Perhaps the finest Florentine sculpture gallery stands out in the open, and there's not even an admission charge. At the *Loggia dei Lanzi,* you are surrounded by works by great artists such as Giambologna, and Cellini, but also ancient sculptures of women → p. 34

● *Fantastic view*

Bus route 12 takes you up the long winding road lined with trees to *Piazzale Michelangelo* where a replica of Michelangelo's David is standing. Take in the breath-taking panoramic view of the city and the Arno valley below for free → p. 61

● *Fuochi di San Giovanni*

Since the 14th century, Florence has celebrated its patron saint on 24 June. To mark the occasion, the city puts on a fabulous *firework display* for its residents and guests below the Piazzale Michelangelo → p. 114

(**I I O O** Dots in guidebook refer to "Best of..." tips

Ponte Vecchio

The Old Bridge is at its most beautiful when the city lights reflected in the Arno compete with the sparkle of the jewellery in the tiny shops on the bridge → p. 40

Uffizi

Offices *(uffizi)* to accommodate the regional administration: that was Vasari's original brief when Cosimo I commissioned the building in 1559. Today, the *Galleria degli Uffizi* is famous the world over → p. 32

Captivating scents

Opened in 1612, the *Officina Profumo-Farmaceutica di Santa Maria Novella* (photo) is an institution in Florence but one which today resembles more of a luxurious perfume store than a monastery apothecary. A unique experience → p. 77

Sweeten your day

The *Café Rivoire* has always been a good place to immerse yourself in Florentine life. Come here to see and be seen – and drink the best hot chocolate in town → p. 64

Gelato artigianale

From simple dealer in dairy produce to world-famous ice cream parlour: Despite stiff competition, *Vivoli* is still the Florentine ice cream parlour par excellence! The ice cream is made to traditional recipes and is exported on special occasions from the heart of Florence even as far as Australia → p. 66

Sandwich alla Fiorentina

A trip to Florence would not be complete without an oozing *panino al lampredotto* or a *trippa alla fiorentina* eaten at one of the traditional food stalls → p. 71

Scale Brunelleschi's dome

It is 116.5 m/382 ft in height and still dominates the city skyline. If you can talk yourself into tackling the arduous climb up to the *dome*, you will be richly rewarded with the chance to see the 16th-century frescoes close up → p. 30

ONLY IN

BEST OF...

● *A culinary festival*
Wander around the mass of stalls selling delicious specialities on the ground floor of the *Mercato Centrale.* Head to the first floor's buzzing food hall for the finest street food → p. 80

● *Oasis of tranquillity*
Take in your impressions of the *Museo degli Innocenti* over a cappuccino on the museum's partly-covered terrace: From up here, the view of the cathedral is one of the most spectacular in Florence → p. 43

● *Seven museums under one roof*
At one time, the Grand Dukes of the Medici family – and for a short period also the Italian royal family – lived here. Today, the *Palazzo Pitti* contains seven of the city's most famous museums → p. 56

● *Countryside in the rain*
The Tuscan landscape can be charming, even in rainy weather; for example when you look at it through the picture windows of the restaurant *Omero,* over a delicious *bistecca alla fiorentina* → p. 67

● *Dazzling colours on dull days*
On entering the salesroom of the *Antico Setificio Fiorentino,* you will be overwhelmed by the glow and sparkle of the fabrics on display: velvet, silk, brocade and taffeta in every possible colour (photo) → p. 76

● *Art in the Renaissance palace*
Regardless of whether it's modern art or the old masters, the exhibitions in the fine rooms of the *Palazzo Strozzi* are always of the highest quality → p. 37

● *Symbol of Florentine power*
The *cathedral* is still one of the largest churches in the world with a truly stunning interior – come rain or shine → p. 30

RAIN

RELAX AND CHILL OUT
Take it easy and spoil yourself

● *Modern spa in an old Palazzo*
SoulSpace is an elegant, stylish spa in the Palazzo Galletti. Treat your-self to an aroma massage or a hot stone day. A Hammam bath and a pool round off the total relaxation package → p. 36

● *Break with a view*
High above the busy Piazza della Repubblica you can recover from all that shopping stress over a cappuccino or a snack on the roof terrace of the *Rinascente* department store → p. 76

● *Soothing waters in the Giardino di Boboli*
The hectic pace of the city is forgotten in an instant when you stroll in the *Giardino di Boboli* to the sound of splashing fountains, on shady paths between statues, nymphs and grottos (photo) → p. 54

● *Monks' chanting*
The atmosphere in the *San Miniato al Monte* church high above the city is one of reflection and becomes positively meditative if you visit at around 5.30 pm. At this time, you can hear the Gregorian vespers chants coming from the neighbouring monastery → p. 61

● *An excursion to the small neighbour*
Take bus 7 for a relaxing journey to *Fiesole* from where you are treated to tranquil views over Florence. Chances are that the views from the San Francesco Monastery will stay with you forever → p. 105

● *Aromatherapy in the park*
In the summer, when the huge wisteria pergola is clad in blossom and the scent of iris, azaleas and hydrangeas captivates your senses, a stroll through the *Giardino Bardini* is as good as any aromatherapy session → p. 55

● *Refuel your energy*
After a day spent walking, you can relax, free your mind and refuel your energy levels in the wellness and beauty spa at the central *Golden Tower Hotel* → p. 36

INTRODUCTION

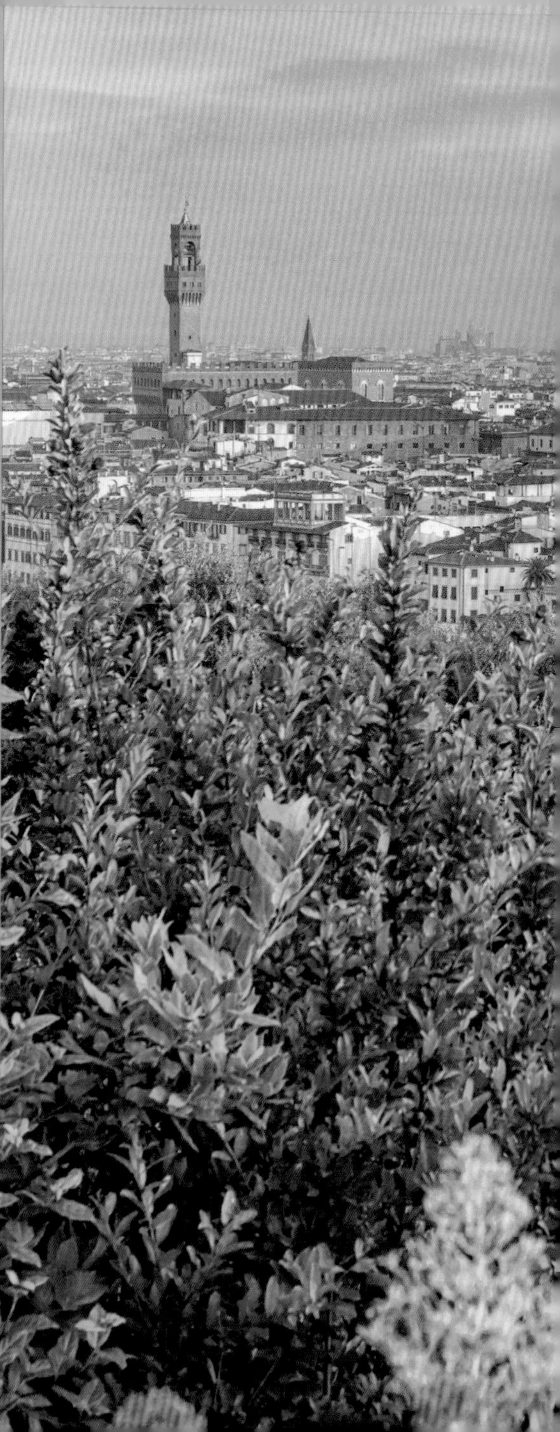

DISCOVER FLORENCE!

The crowds. Not to be avoided in the medieval lanes of this compact city. Yet how could the city planners all those years ago have guessed that the city would one day be overrun by 5 million tourists a year? And they know what to expect: Florence is a miniature metropolis and one of the most beautiful cities in the world. Young and old, singles and couples, art lovers, gourmets, shopaholics and globetrotters – everyone loves Florence!

Florence has something for everyone, regardless of interests or tastes. Young people soak up the sun on the squares and gather round to listen to street musicians in the evening, stand around chatting outside the *bars and trattorias*, or party in the clubs. Gourmets throng the restaurants and enoteche (wine bars) to make their informed selection of ham, cheese, wine and olive oil. Well-to-do Asians, Americans and Europeans gladly bear the burden of their purchases, acquired on the *elegant shopping streets*. And, sooner or later, they all end up together in the queue to get into the Uffizi Gallery, the Palazzo Pitti or the Galleria dell'Accademia. After all, Florence is all about art. The ensemble of churches and palaces, squares and alleyways, fountains and statues is a *gigantic work of art, which has grown over centuries* and

---

is unequalled the world over. The finest sculptures, paintings and tapestries are on display in the churches and over 70 museums in the city.

The palaces have been transformed by generations of residents into *veritable treasure chambers*, the majority *surrounded by magnificent gardens*. Many of them are open to the public. Every palace door, window ledge or roof gutter is a work of art in its own right. Almost all major sights are easily reached on foot. Be courageous and turn a corner into one of the side streets or tiny alleyways either side of the main thoroughfares. You will discover much that is beautiful and interesting – things which don't even get a mention in the travel guides! The city centre is small. But if you should ever get lost, you can ask any Florentine the way to the *duomo*, the cathedral. It is never far away – and, before you know it, you are back among the tourist masses once again!

> **Every window ledge, every roof gutter is a work of art in its own right**

Florence's situation is without equal. The River Arno flows through the centre of the city, and the surrounding hills are dotted with spectacular *villas encircled by cypress*

The narrow lanes suddenly open up to the wide, open space of the Piazza S. Croce

trees. In winter and spring you can see the snow-capped peaks of the Pratomagno and the Apennines to the east and north of the city. During the building boom of recent years, wise urban planners have seen to it that the centuries-old face of the city has not changed too much. Today, only a small proportion of the 382,000 inhabitants of Florence actually live in the centre, as housing prices are among the highest in Italy. You are more likely to meet Florentines here on their way to work or – a rare enough occurrence – shopping in the expensive boutiques.

Centuries-old cityscape

Today, the heart of the city is in the hand of the tourists; Florence has little industry and lives to a large extent from its foreign guests. Numbers of visitors have risen again in the last few years, since now the Chinese, Indians, Russians and Eastern Europeans have discovered the city as a holiday destination. In 2017, almost *14.5 million overnight stays* were registered in Florence province! On average, tourists stay in the city for three days – enough time to put together a varied programme including the most important sights yet still leaving room to soak up the city's flair. Don't rush things: plan to look at only one of the large museums and no more than

two churches per day, to allow time for just strolling along and taking in your surroundings. And then look forward to the evenings, when you can savour the *famous Tuscan cuisine* and the region's no less famous wines at one of the many trattorias and restaurants.

What makes Florence so fascinating is, above all, its wealth of *unique artistic and architectural treasures*. There is scarcely another place in which so many world-famous artists have lived and worked. It is almost impossible to list all the painters, sculptors, architects, poets and philosophers who have helped to shape the face of the city down the centuries and thus contributed to its fame. The first artistic highpoint was during the 14th and 15th centuries, when Dante wrote his *Divine Comedy* and Giotto, Orcagna and Masaccio painted their stunning frescoes in the churches. Brunelleschi built the magnificent cathedral dome and Alberti formulated the theoretical principles of Renaissance art. Many others were to follow; the city flourished once again in the 16th century, thanks to the activities of *Michelangelo, Raphael and Vasari*.

At the height of its fortunes in the Middle Ages, Florence influenced politics, trade and art in the whole of Europe. Even then, the city was able to look back on more than 2,000 years of history. Archaeological discoveries prove that a settlement must have existed here as early as the Villanova era around 1000 BC. In 59 BC, the Romans founded a veterans' colony in the Arno valley which they called *Florentia*. The forum was on the same spot as the Piazza della Repubblica today. The Romans were succeeded by the Lombards and the Carolingians, and in the year 845 AD, Lothar, grandson of Charlemagne, united the earldoms of Florence and Fiesole. Back in 1115, Florence was to all intents and purposes already an autonomous community, and the foundations for its *rise to glory* had already been laid. The Baptistery and the San Miniato and Santissimi Apostoli churches were built and from the 13th century onwards, Florence developed into a major European trading centre.

Bankers in Florence financed popes and kings

The city had become rich and powerful, not least thanks to its *flourishing textile trade* and the minting of the *fiorino* in 1252. This first gold coin was to become the principle means of payment in the whole of Europe. The *banking system* as we know it today also has its roots in Florence. The *banco*, or money lenders' table, gave rise to the term "bank", and it was in Florence that the first bills of exchange and cheques were issued. Florentine bankers financed the activities of popes and kings. In the city itself, a veritable building boom ensued, as churches and palaces sprang up everywhere. In 1296 the ruling council of this city-state of 100,000 inhabitants decided to build the mighty cathedral.

At around this time, the rise began of the family which was destined to control the fate of the city for the next 300 years: the *Medici*. Their wealth and their appreciation and sponsorship of the arts determined to a considerable extent the development and appearance of the city. Florence owes the Medici many of its most important buildings, for example, the Palazzo Medici Riccardi, residence of Cosimo il Vecchio (the Elder) with its wonderful Gozzoli Chapel. Similarly, the Basilica San Lorenzo, including the Cappella dei Principi, the family mausoleum which is entirely decorated in frescoes and semi-precious stones. The Galleria degli Uffizi, too, with its world-famous collection of paintings or the Palazzo Pitti and the treasures it contains are the fruits of Medici patronage. The spectacular *Medici villas in the immediate vicinity* of the city are crowd-pullers to this day. And it was a woman, Anna Maria Luisa (1667–1743), the last of this powerful dynasty, who laid down in her will that, "of the things which are for the decoration of the city, for the benefit of the public or a source of curiosity for outsiders (!), none should ever be sold or removed from the confines of the Grand Duchy". As if she had foreseen the attraction the city would exert and the significance of the collections as a source of revenue in the future. But

Both locals and tourists squeeze up together for lunch at Nerbone

in 1737, the Grand Duchy of Tuscany fell to the house of Habsburg-Lorraine, which ruled the region, apart from a short Napoleonic intermezzo (1799–1815) until 1859.

Between 1865 and 1871 Florence was the *capital of the newly founded kingdom*, the beginning of a second Renaissance. To underline the city's new prominence, the buildings in the old market quarter and the medieval ghetto were torn down to make way for the Piazza della Repubblica. The city wall was razed to the ground and the broad ring road constructed in its place – still one of the most important thoroughfares. Bourgeois quarters were founded outside this former city boundary.

For many years, the city lived almost exclusively from the prestige of its past. Increasingly, however, modernity is gaining a foothold. Many of the more recent exhibitions focus on the *present or future*. There is a sense of "blowing away the cobwebs" and daring to be a little more experimental. Nowadays, anything goes – from avant-garde theatre to diverse performances – and is actively encouraged. The historic squares form the stunning backdrop to *modern installations and street festivals*. Considering the degree of artistic sensitivity the city has developed down the centuries, the Florence is sure to keep on thrilling its visitors in the future. After all, Florence is a metropolis – albeit a small one – but one with class and flair. And it's fun – for everyone!

Modernity with a historical backdrop

WHAT'S HOT

1 Coffee culture

More than just beans In some cafés in the city you can also take in a vernissage, book presentation or a bit of theatre. The *La Cité Libreria Café (Mon–Sat 9am–2am, Sun from 3pm | Borgo San Frediano 20r | www.lacitelibreria.info)* is known for its book selection and cabaret shows. In contrast, *Todo Modo (Tue–Sun 10am–8pm | Via dei Fossi 15r | www.todomodo.org)* is a laid-back café-bistrot, with cool wine bar and cosy bookshop offering a varied program of cultural events.

Urban beach

2

Easy living alongside the Arno Open from May to September, *Florence's city beach (Piazza Giuseppe Poggi | www.easylivingfirenze.it) (photo)* is a great place to relax and unwind on one of the many deckchairs, with yoga by sunset on Wednesdays at 7.30pm and panini and salads served at the beach bar. Or enjoy the mild summer evenings with a cocktail hour followed by live DJs for guests to party into the night.

Santo Spirito

3

The two faces of Santo Spirito Alongside old, established craft workshops, you'll find cool galleries and shops. Start your tour of the neighbourhood at the *Centro Machiavelli (Piazza Santo Spirito 4 | www.centromachiavelli.it)*, where shoes and mosaics are still produced by hand. Up-to-the-minute creations are the speciality of the three sisters at *Quelle Tre (Via Santo Spirito 42r | www.quelletre.it)*. In their atelier, they sell quirky clothes and accessories. After your successful foray to the shops, your meal on the wooden benches at the *Osteria Santo Spirito (Piazza Santo Spirito 16r | tel. 05 52 38 23 83 | www.osteriasantospirito.it)*, with a view over the market, tastes twice as good.

City gardeners & eco chefs

Green is the colour Florence used to be known for its poor air quality. For some years now, the city's "green lung" has been getting larger, thanks also to the ◉ *Guerilla Gardeners (www.guerrillagardener.it)*. They have taken it into their own hands to make the city greener and are campaigning for mobile gardens on the Via dell'Agnolo and the Piazza Tasso. Fancy a "green" holiday in Florence? Hire an environmentally friendly ◉ *Pedicab (www.pedicabfirenze.it)* and round off your eco-sightseeing tour with a visit to ◉ *La Raccolta (Via Giacomo Leopardi 2r | www.laraccolta.it | Moderate–Expensive)*. This eco-restaurant has some of the most delicious food in town. At ◉ *EcoPopup (Via del Giglio 27r | www.ecopopup.it)* you can buy cool organic clothing and gifts.

4

Midnight cravings

Early bird catches the croissants Florentines know where to get their hands on the best freshly-baked pastries if hunger strikes in the night. Open until 3am, the *Bobo Check Point (Piazza Ferrucci)* kiosk in the San Niccolò quarter sells delicious Nutella croissants. The *Re della Foresta (until 3am, Sun until 5am | Piazza Giorgini 22/r)* keeps a constant supply of tasty brioches coming from its oven for early morning delivery to the local bars. In the Santa Croce district, sweet smells hang in the air between 11pm and 4am around the *Pasticceria Vinci & Bongini (Via Canto Rivolto)* and the ever-overcrowded *Pastaio (Via Campo d'Arrigo 14r)* close to the stadium is an absolute hotspot, often already sold out by 3am.

5

IN A NUTSHELL

THE CHINESE ARE COMING

Florence doesn't have its own China-town yet, but more than 22,000 Chinese now live permanently in Florence. The city also attracts 4.2 million tourists from China every year and natives of this Far East country are well and truly part of the fabric of the city. The Chinese tourists have a taste (and a wallet) for luxury and love the major Italian fashion labels. Often loaded down by their mountains of shopping bags, they can be seen dragging their purchases back to their hotels across the city's squares. However, this image is a far cry from the Chinese population which lives in the city. They struggle to make ends meet by opening new mini shops

all over the city selling cheap goods which in turn pose a threat to the long-established traders. Colourful clothes hang in front of these shops, enticing shoppers inside to purchase discount merchandise. Most of the textiles are made by Chinese sweat-shop workers in Prato, 20 km/12.5 miles from Florence. By estimates, every fifth inhabitant of this town with an overall population of 200,000 comes from China. They work 16 to 17-hour days, sometimes eating and sleeping in the factory under the worst conditions. In 2017, there were over 5000 of these "textile factories" registered in Prato. However, this is definitely the place to come if you're looking for that authentic Chinese dining experience: Visitors could be mis-

Aspects of a multi-faceted city – interesting facts about the Medici, Calcio in Costume or the Chinese

taken for thinking they were in the land of the dragon.

CONTEMPORARY BEHIND THE ANCIENT FACADE

Perhaps Florence isn't the first city that comes to mind when you think of contemporary art. Yet he who looks will find. Today, the city boasts many modern sculptures; you will be greeted at the airport by Fernando Botero's bulbous sparrow, Henry Moore's "Warri-or with Shield" stands in the monastery courtyard of S. Croce and the Belgian sculptor Jean-Michel Folon showcases many of his sculptures around the city. Florence's galleries host exhibitions of contemporary art throughout the year, focusing on modern paintings as well as sculpture, video installations, visual poetry and lots more besides. Many galleries have modern art for sale and the new Museo del Novecento offers a fusion of contemporary art and Renaissance Florence. True fans of contemporary art should take a trip to the neighbouring town of Prato, home to the Museo Pecci, one of Italy's most interesting and influential modern art museums.

FINE FEATHERS MAKE FINE BIRDS

Italian fashion conquered the world thanks to the city of Florence. It all started in 1951 when Conte Gian Battista Giorgini organised the first fashion show for a small circle of friends to take their minds off the war around them. This event caused a real stir internationally and paved the way for the annual fashion shows held annually in the Palazzo Pitti. The hub of Italian women's fashion has now moved to Milan, though Italian menswear is still successfully presented in Florence in January and June at the "Pitti Uomo" fair *(www.pittimmagine. com)* held in the Fortezza da Basso.

HAVE MERCY UPON US

Plagued on holiday with a cough, cold or sore throat? Don't worry, misericordia (mercy) is never far away, namely on the cathedral square. Florentine doctors in all fields of medicine work in the outpatient clinic at the *Fratellanza della Misericordia (Vicolo degli Adimari 1 | surgery hours for tourists Mon–Fri 2pm–4pm)* – for a pittance of a pay. A real blessing not only for the city's poorer residents, but for many a distressed tourist too. This compassionate brotherhood was founded in Florence in 1244. The *fratelli* (brothers) devoted themselves from the very beginning to the care of the sick and poor and the transport of the deceased. They worked day and night, dressed in black cassocks with large hoods pulled down over their heads revealing only their eyes to guarantee their anonymity. The medieval cassocks were replaced by orange outfits in 2006 which the *fratelli*

SPOTLIGHT ON SPORTS

Almost all Florentines are *tifosi*, fans of the football team A.C.F. Fiorentina *(it. violachannel.tvt)*. Home games take place every other Sunday (info: *www. fiorentina.it)*. Tickets can be bought directly at the stadium *Stadio Comunale Artemio Franchi* **(135 E4)** *(ĵ K3) (Mon–Fri 10am–7pm, Sun from 5pm before the game | Via dei Sette Santi/Via Dupré | tel. 05 57 12 59)* or at the *Mercato Centrale* **(130 B–C1)** *(ĵ F4) (Mon–Sat 10am–2pm and 3–7.30pm | Piazza del Meracto Centrale | tel. 05 52 74 11 49)*. Important: For security reasons, tickets are only sold upon presentation of your passport or identity card!

The horse racing track *Ippodromo del Visarno* **(132 A4–5)** *(ĵ B3) (www. visarno.it)* is located in Florence's city park, the *Parco delle Cascine.* You can find all the important information on upcoming events on the internet – where you can also sign up for the horse races.
Some 30 km/18.5 miles north of Florence, in the heart of the *Mugello,* is the motor racing circuit of the same name. The Grand Prix, the *Gran Premio d'Italia,* is held here every year, as is the *Formula 3000* race *(tel. 05 58 49 91 11 | www. mugellocircuit.it)*. Tickets in advance from *www.ticketone.it*.

Patchwork eye-catcher! Florence is still a hotbed of fashion

now wear while they wait next to their modern ambulances parked in front of the headquarters on the Piazza del Duomo. A small museum inside the building vividly documents the history of the misericordia.

MAN, THE MEASURE OF ALL THINGS: THE RENAISSANCE

The originals of everything you learnt at school or have googled about this period of art (approx. 1420–1600) can be seen in Florence, the birthplace of the Renaissance. The city is full of world-class and timeless examples from science, art and architecture, ranging from the scientific enlightenment of Leonardo Da Vinci and Galileo Galilei at the Museo Galileo, the new architecture exhibited by Brunelleschi in the cathedral's dome or by Leon Battista Alberti in the Palazzo Rucellai, or Sandro Bot-ticelli's divine painting at the Uffizi. The iconic masterpiece of the Renaissance's greatest genius, Michelangelo's David, is not only on display in the original, it also features on all kinds of souvenirs. It's no surprise then that Florence is known as the "cradle of the Renaissance" and home to the rebirth of Antiquity. The Renaissance captured the zeitgeist of its time: In contrast to the medieval period, man was placed at the centre of the universe – a philosophy which became manifest in the city's art, architecture, politics, science and literature.

MODERN DAY GLADIATORS

Hard to believe but even Emilio Pucci, the right honourable citizen of Florence and internationally acclaimed fashion designer, was seen not too many years ago rolling around in mud at this historical footballing event, the *Calcio in Costume.* The Florentines are avid football fans – a passion dating back to the 16th century. Held in June every year on the Piazza Santa Croce (which is covered in a makeshift field of sand), this unique spectacle is organised by two of the city's historical districts and involves 54 inhabitants dressing up in medieval costume; the final always takes place on June 24, to celebrate the city's patron San Giovanni. Every year you notice how times – and the rules – have changed with regard to the calcio today; the boundless enthusiasm of the Florentines for the *Calcio in Costume*, however, has not lessened down the centuries *(www.calciostoricofioretino.it).*

THEY RULED AND THEY BUILT

Florence can count their lucky stars. If it hadn't been for an amazing lady, the city's art treasures would have been spread around the world, the authorities would have made themselves at home in the Uffizi and the Palazzo Pitti would have been converted into living quarters. Anna Maria Luisa de' Medici (1667–1743) avoided all of these monstrosities from happening. In her will, she left all her family's belongings and treasures to the city of Florence to prevent them going to auction. A pretty statue and a modest inscription on the San Lorenzo Church thank her for her generosity. She was the last in line of the amazing Medici family.

The Medicis attained their wealth through banking. They governed over the city for decades and, thanks to their clever politics, appreciation and sponsorship of the arts determined to a considerable extent the appearance of this beautiful city. They built monumental palaces, spectacular villas, bridges and churches and promoted the artists of their generation. Especially the "Father of the Renaissance",

COURSES FOR ALL INTERESTS

Whether it's language, painting, ceramics or the art of cooking, the range of courses on offer is extremely varied. *Florenceart* **(137 D4)** *(⚏ E4) (Via della Scala 11 | www.florenceart.net)* offers short decorative painting and trompe l'oeil courses. There's a huge selection of courses, too, at the *Florence Academy of Art* **(138 B3)** *(⚏ H5) (Via delle Casine 21r | www.florenceacademyofart. com).* An excellent place to learn various graphic-art techniques is *Il Bisonte* **(138 B4)** *(⚏ G6) (Via San Niccolò 24r | www.ilbisonte.it).* At the famous school *Palazzo Spinelli* **(137 E3)** *(⚏ E6) (Istituto per l'Arte e il Restauro | Via Maggio 13 | www.spinelli.it)* you can take summer courses and learn the craft of restoring different materials. *Le Arti Orafe* **(137 D3)** *(⚏ E6) (Via dei Serragli 104–124 | www. artiorafe.it)* rates as the best goldsmith's school far and wide. If you are interested in fashion, take a summer course at the renowned *Polimoda* **(137 D2)** *(⚏ D4)* school *(Villa Favard | Via del Curtatone 1 | www.polimoda.com).* At *Cordon Bleu* **(131 F1)** *(⚏ H4) (Via di Mezzo 55r | www.cordonbleu-it.com)* they'll let you into the secrets of the art of good cooking. Brush up your Italian at *Italian Me* **(130 B4)** *(⚏ F5) (Via Tornabuoni 1 | www.italianme.it)* and at the *Istituto Il David* **(130 B3)** *(⚏ F5) (Via Vecchietti 1 | www.davidschool.com).*

Cosimo Il Vecchio (1389–1464), profited from their generosity. No less famous is his grandson Lorenzo (1449–92) who was given the nickname "il Magnifico" due to his affluent lifestyle and success: He died at just 42 years of age but had already managed in his 23 years of reign to conquer almost the entire region of Tuscany and transform Florence into the spiritual actually "invented" in Florence. The story goes like this: Although crushed ice had been added to drinks in summer months as far back as Ancient times, it took centuries – and the brainwave of an ingenious lady – before the *gelato* conquered the world as a sweet dessert. Unsurprisingly, a member of the Medici family again had a hand in its invention; this

The arcade courtyard of the Medici Palazzo is testimony to the Medici family's love of art

and cultural hub of Europe. Would today's politicians manage such a feat?

WE ALL SCREAM FOR ICE CREAM

Tucked away behind the Piazza Santa Croce is one of Florence's best ice-cream parlours, *Vivoli geletaria* – just head towards the crowds of people devouring ice cream. This *gelateria* is still one of the best addresses in Florence for fans of gelato. Not quite so well-known is the fact that ice cream, as we know it today, was

time Caterina de' Medici (1519–89), an enthusiastic cook who, after her marriage to the French Dauphin, introduced the Florentine cuisine to France. But before leaving Florence, she held a competition for the "the most exciting dish which had ever been created". The winner was a poultry dealer and hobby food inventor with his *gelato*. She then took the ice cream with her to France. And the rest is history. Today, ice cream parlours such as Vivoli send their ice cream creations as far away as Australia for special occasions.

SIGHTSEEING

CITY **WHERE TO START?**
Ponte Vecchio (130 B–C5)
(*F5*): Stand on the famous Arno bridge and get your bearings; heading out of town, you come to the mighty Palazzo Pitti and the Via Maggio with its many antique dealers. On the other side of the river you can see the Uffizi. Behind them come the Piazza della Signoria with the city landmark, the Palazzo Vecchio, and a little to the northeast, the Piazza della Repubblica and the Piazza del Duomo. Electric minibuses C3 and D; car parking at the Stazione Santa Maria Novella.

Florence is best explored on foot – no problem, since almost all the sights are within the square mile of the city centre! The museum landscape in Florence is infinitely varied: Besides the universally acclaimed art collections at the Uffizi and the Palazzo Pitti, it's worth taking a look at the Museo Nazionale del Bargello and the Galleria dell'Accademia, which house important sculptures, as well as the host of museums scattered across the city dedicated to science and other disciplines.

You can get an overall idea of the state museums and what they have to offer from *www.polomuseale.firenze.it*, while *www.museivicifiorentini.comune.fi.it* has information on the municipal museums.

Photo: Galleria degli Uffizi

Art, as far as the eye can see –
blockbuster museums, glorious churches and
fabulous palaces await your visit

To avoid long queues, reserve admission tickets to the state museums in advance *(at least 5 days before your visit! at www. firenzemusei.it or tel. 0 55 29 48 83 | booking fee: approx. 4–5 euros, for special exhibitions, add another 3 euros).* The churches are usually open from 8am–12:30pm and 3pm or 4pm–6pm. Admission to churches, museums and parks is generally no longer possible 30–60 minutes before closing time. INSIDER TIP▶ Have a handful of coins at the ready: you'll need them to feed the "talking info posts" and to switch on the floodlights in the chapels!

SOUTHERN SAN GIOVANNI

The area between the Duomo and Palazzo Vecchio, the seat of local government, is the centre of the city. Where

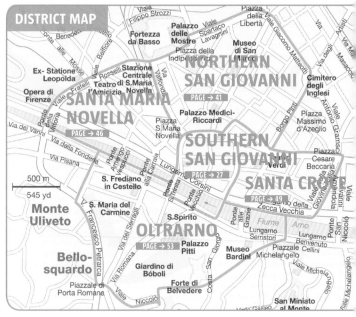

DISTRICT MAP

The map shows the location of the most interesting districts. There is a detailed map of each district on which each of the sights described is numbered.

Romans once marched along the Cardo Maximus, hordes of tourists jostle along today's Via Calzaiuoli.

Since time immemorial, this street full of fashion boutiques and shoe shops, ice cream parlours and obligatory pizzerias, has linked the spiritual and profane sides of the city. This is the nerve-centre of Florence, and everyone passes this way – even the hastiest tourist.

■ BATTISTERO DI SAN GIOVANNI (130 C3) (*ш F4*)

"This is the gate to paradise!" is what Michelangelo supposedly exclaimed when he saw the golden portal leading into the baptistery. It took 26 years (1426-1452) for Lorenzo Ghiberti to complete the double door fac-

ing the cathedral, the so-called *Door of Paradise,* after he had finished the north portal a few years before. The bald-headed figure in the right-hand column of the door's left wing is a self-portrait of Ghiberti. The southern door, illustrating the life of John the Baptist, was executed in 1336 by Andrea Pisano.

Next to the cathedral, this octagonal baptistery with its elegant white and green marble *cladding* appears miniscule in size: Its 25.6m/83ft diameter is just half the size of the Cathedral's entire dome. Its first mention in a document as a "church" dates back to 897 yet its origins as a place of worship probably go back even further. The inside of the baptistery is equally divine.

The glistening, **INSIDER TIP** *mosaic-covered* interior of the octagonal dome is crowned by a gigantic figure of Christ (around 1270) above the apse. The walls are covered in numerous works of art. *Mon–Fri 8.15am–10.15 am and 11.15am–6.30pm, Sat 8.15am–6.30pm, Sun 8.15am–1.30pm | admission (joint ticket including cathedral, crypt, dome, campanile and museum) 10 euros | Piazza di San Giovanni | www.ilgrandemuseodelduomo.it*

■2■ CASA DI DANTE (131 D4) (*ΩΩ F5*)

If he had never met his Beatrice, who knows if Dante would have resided so long in Florence between the fighting enemy groups? Everything what we know about the greatest Italian poet (1265–1321) is documented in this small museum, housed in what is assumed to be Dante's birthplace. *Nov–March Tue–Sun 10am–5pm, April–Oct daily 10am–6pm | admission 4 euros | Via Santa Margherita 1 | www.museocasadidante.it*

■3■ CORRIDOIO VASARIANO (130 B–C 5–6) (*ΩΩ F5–6*)

Throughout the ages, security has been a top priority among the rich and famous, and combined with ingenuity, it can produce something really special such as the Vasari Corridor. This narrow 1 km/0.6 mile-long covered passageway was designed to allow the Medici family to wander in privacy and safety around the city between the government offices in the Palazzo Vecchio to the family's former palace, the Palazzo Pitti. The corridor passes along the Uffizi, across the Ponte Vecchio above the shops below, continues inside the Santa Felicita church and ends at the Palazzo Pitti in the Giardino di Boboli near the Buontalenti grotto. In 1565, Grand Duke Cosimo I de' Medici commissioned Giorgio Vasari to build this corridor which took him a mere 5 months to complete. Today, the walls of the corridor are mostly covered in self-portraits of Italian artists. *Reservation well in advance | Piazzale degli Uffizi 6 | tel. 05 52 38 86 21 | www.uffizi.it*

⭐ **Duomo & Campanile**
Unimaginable: the richness of the cathedral interior; unrivalled: the view from the dome or the bell tower → p. 30

⭐ **Galleria degli Uffizi**
Over 39 rooms encompassing a world-famous collection of paintings → p. 32

⭐ **Palazzo Vecchio**
Impressive interiors from the city's heyday → p. 38

⭐ **Ponte Vecchio**
The famous bridge is best seen when illuminated at night → p. 40

⭐ **Galleria dell'Accademia**
Michelangelo's David and a sublime collection of late Gothic art → p. 41

⭐ **San Lorenzo**
The Medicis had their funerary chapels designed by famous artists → p. 45

⭐ **Museo Nazionale del Bargello**
Sculpture museum in a former prison → p. 51

⭐ **Santa Croce**
The Pantheon of Florence → p. 52

⭐ **Giardino di Boboli**
Green oasis behind the Palazzo Pitti → p. 54

⭐ **San Miniato al Monte**
A saint enthroned above the city → p. 61

MARCO POLO HIGHLIGHTS

4 DUOMO DI SANTA MARIA DEL FIORE & CAMPANILE ★ ●
(130–131 C–D3) (*M* F–G4)

The massive cupola of the *cathedral* dominates the Florence skyline for miles. Its construction was a belated triumph, since Pisa, Lucca, Pistoia, Prato and Siena already had their own magnificent cathedrals by the time Florence city council finally got round to commissioning the building of this one in 1296. The task was assigned to Arnolfo di Cambio, and the gigantic project was completed in 1368, admittedly without the ● *cupola*. It was only in 1420–34 that this was added by Filippo Brunelleschi. The planned diameter of the dome was over 45 m/148 ft and presented considerable, hitherto unknown constructional challenges. Brunelleschi's concept was based essentially on the fact that bodies which lean towards each other support each other too. He therefore built inner and outer concentric domes resting on the drum of the cathedral. If you feel up to it, climb the 463 steps up to the ☼ lantern through the nave and the double-walled cupola – the same route taken by the construction workers of old! (Caution: one-way system – it's not possible to turn around and go back!) On the way, you get a fascinating insight into the INSIDERTIP "innards" of the dome – and ultimately an amazing view of the city!

Florence Cathedral is the fourth-largest church in Christendom. Its surface area is 8300 m² (9926.9 yd²), at a length of 160 m (175 yd). Many renowned Florentine artists contributed at the time to its decoration. The large fresco (the second on the left-hand side) shows the equestrian statue of mercenary leader Sir John Hawkwood, who once triumphed in battle for the city. It was painted in 1436 by Paolo Uccello and served as the model for all subsequent works of its kind. The painting of the equestrian statue of Niccolò da Tolentino next to it is by Andrea del Castagno (1456). The circular

Towering above the roofs of Florence: the cathedral's dome and Giotto's Campanile

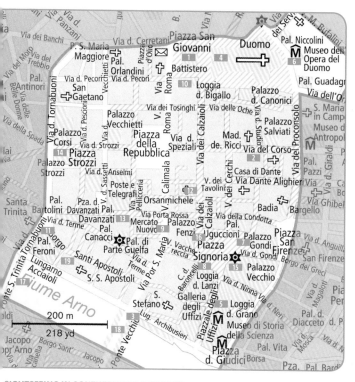

SIGHTSEEING IN SOUTHERN SAN GIOVANNI

1. Battistero di San Giovanni
2. Casa di Dante
3. Corrridoio Vasariano
4. Duomo di Santa Maria del Fiore & Campanile
5. Galleria degli Uffizi
6. Grande Museo del Duomo
7. Gucci Garden
8. Loggia dei Lanzi
9. Loggia del Mercato Nuovo
10. Museo del Bigallo
11. Museo Salvatore Ferragamo
12. Orsanmichele
13. Palazzo Davanzati

Pedestrian precinct
14. Palazzo Strozzi
15. Palazzo Vecchio
16. Piazza della Signoria
17. Ponte Santa Trinita
18. Ponte Vecchio
19. Santissimi Apostoli

stained-glass windows in the drum at the base of the dome were designed by major artists of the 14th century. The inside of the dome was embellished with frescos depicting the *Last Judgement* by Giorgio Vasari and Federico Zuccari between 1572 and 1579. The colourful, glazed *terracotta reliefs* above the entrances to the two Sacristies are by Luca della Robbia (1444–69), as is the *bronze door* to the New Sacristy to the left of the high altar. The famous cantorias ("singing galleries") by Donatello and Luca della Robbia as well as the *Pietà* by Michelangelo can now be seen in the *Grande Museo del Duomo* (see p. 34).

31

SOUTHERN SAN GIOVANNI

A staircase to the right of the main entrance leads down into the remains of the Early Christian church of *Santa Reparata*, which pre-dates the cathedral and which was uncovered in 1966. It contains the tomb of Brunelleschi, among others. In 2000, a skeleton found there was identified conclusively as that of Giotto (1267–1337), which was then laid to rest next to Brunelleschi. The exterior of the cathedral is clad in white Carrara marble and green marble from Prato. The front section of the façade was only completed in 1887 in the neo-Gothic style.

artists such as Donatello (the originals are also in the Museo dell'Opera). 414 comfortable steps lead up to the balustrade of the flat roof and to a fabulous panorama. *Duomo and Santa Reparata crypt: Mon–Wed, Fri 10am–5pm, Thu 10am–4.30pm, Sat 10am–4.45pm, Sun 1.30pm–4.45pm; closed 1st Tue of the month; dome: Mon–Fri 8.30am–7pm, Sat 8.30am–5pm, Sun 1pm–4pm; campanile: daily 8.15am–7pm | admission: joint ticket 15 euros | www.operaduomo. firenze.it*

Its humble beginnings! The octagonal tribuna of the Uffizi

Directly next to the cathedral stands the ⚜ *campanile* (bell tower), which was designed by Giotto and built between 1334 and 1359. Due to his harmonious proportions and use of colour, it rates as one of the most beautiful in Italy. Its façade features encrustations of white, red and green marble. The lower section has 54 bas-reliefs from the school of Andrea Pisano; in the niches above stand statues of the saints, prophets and sibyls by

5 GALLERIA DEGLI UFFIZI ★ ●
(130 C5) (*F5*)
Commissioned by Cosimo I de' Medici, the building was constructed according to plans by Giorgio Vasari between 1559 and 1581 to house the city's administrative offices. Meanwhile, it is home to one of the richest and most fabled painting collections in the world as well as, on the first floor, the *Gabinetto dei Disegni e delle Stampe*, a collection of 150,000 drawings

and prints. The floors below are gradually being converted into exhibition space – the *Nuovi Uffizi* ("New Uffizi"). You can follow the progress of this enormous project under *www.nuoviuffizi.it.* Yet having been in storage for decades, over 330 works of art are already on display now for you to appreciate on 3000 m² of newly created exhibition space in many new rooms. The new exhibition concept, modern lighting, restored marble flooring and ceiling designs are in stark contrast to the older rooms. Viewing starts on the second floor, the paintings are arranged chronologically from the 13th to the 15th century and according to schools.

The main emphasis is on the Italian Renaissance. Greek and Roman statues as well as Flemish Gobelin tapestries are to be seen in the corridors. The most valuable statues stand on specially constructed plinths in the *Tribuna del Buontalenti*, the magnificent octagonal room which was one of the first to be conceived as a backdrop for works of art and which can now be admired again after a long time of restoration.

Following the signposts for a suggested tour you come first to the large Gothic altarpieces by Cimabue and Giotto, followed by works from the Sienese school of the 14th century and the great painters of the early Renaissance: Masaccio, Piero della Francesca and also Sandro Botticelli, whose paintings, including *The Birth of Venus*, are displayed in their own room. Leonardo da Vinci's masterpieces on display here include the large *Adoration of the Magi*.

The building's west wing contains works from Titian *(Venus of Urbino),* from the Venetian artists Veronese, Tintoretto and Caravaggio as well as the re-designed room 35, the *Sala Rossa,* in which you can admire among other splendours the Ton-

do Doni, one of Michelangelo's most famous paintings. The first floor belongs to the new section of the Uffizi Gallery. The *Sale Blu,* or blue rooms, are dedicated to the 16th and 17th century Spanish, French, Flemish and Dutch painters (Rubens, Rembrandt and van Dyck). Next, the *Sale Rosse* mainly exhibit paintings from the Florentine Mannerism movement with outstanding works from Andrea del Sarto and Raphael. Other highlights include works by Rosso Fiorentino and Pontormo and the famous Medici portraits by Bronzino. The tour takes you past paintings by Correggio and Parmigianino up to the Venetian school of painting and ends in the *Sale Gialle,* or the yellow rooms, showcasing 17th century works.

LOW BUDGET

Admission charges to museums are relatively high, but EU residents under 25 pay a reduced price in the state museums in Florence; the under 18s get in free (don't forget your ID!).

All state museums in Italy open their doors to the public for free on the first Sunday of every month, an event known as ● *DomenicalMuseo (www. museifirenze.it)* and in spring there is a whole week of free admission. Find out the exact dates at the tourist information.

During the international music festival *Maggio Musicale Fiorentino* in May and June you can sit in for free on the amazing rehearsals in various concert venues, usually on Sunday mornings. More information at *www. maggiofiorentino.com.*

Guided tours of the Uffizi Gallery are also organised. Make sure to plan for a coffee break on the ☕ roof terrace on the second floor so as not to miss the panoramic view! *Tue–Sun 8:15am–6:50pm | admission 8 euros, special exhibitions: 12.50 euros | Piazzale degli Uffizi 6 | www.uffizi.firenze.it*

6 INSIDER TIP GRANDE MUSEO DEL DUOMO (131 D3) (*ΩΩ G4–5*)

Gazing up in awe at Brunelleschi's cathedral dome, you will give little thought to how on earth the thousands of tiles were transported onto the roof. It took centuries for the long-forgotten cathedral workshop to be transformed into today's Museo del Duomo. Where building materials, used to build the cathedral in the 16th century were once stored, stands today Florence's most contemporary and best-designed museum. Light and space are the main elements of this impressive building. An entire hall in this 6000m^2/64,600 sq.ft. of exhibition space is dedicated to Brunelleschi's dome which, once you have ploughed through all the detailed information and artefacts, sheds a completely new light on the architect's ground-breaking dome. The museum tells in minute detail the story of the cupola's construction through photos, artefacts and films. And the same is true for the cathedral itself. The spectacular 20 m/66 ft-high exhibition hall is dominated by a life-size reconstruction of the floral white-marble façade of the cathedral originally designed by the *campanile* architect Arnolfo di Cambio (the cathedral was eventually given a Neo-Gothic façade at the end of the 19th century). Over 700 of the statues carved for the bell tower and inside the duomo as well as other works of art, which had to be taken down from their original position for safety and weather reasons, can be seen here. These include works by Michelangelo, Donatello, Ghiberti and others. There is no better place than here to admire these masterpieces up close and in their full glory. The same applies to the cantorias (singing galleries) by Luca della Robbia as well as to the gloriously golden Doors of Paradise for the Baptistery. *Daily 9am–7pm | admission: joint ticket (museum, duomo, crypta, dome, campanile) 15 euros | Piazza del Duomo 9 | www.ilgrandemuseodelduomo.it*

7 GUCCI GARDEN (131 D4) (*ΩΩ F5*)

Gucci is synonymous with Florentine fashion, style and quality. This three-storey museum tracks the history of this world famous fashion house since it was founded in Florence in 1921. You can also buy really stylish outfits here – if you can afford it. Massimo Bottura, one of the world's most creative chefs, has opened his *Osteria (Expensive)* here in 2018: you can't get more first-class than this! *Fri–Wed 10am–8pm, Thu until 11pm | admission 8 euros, Thu from 8pm 4 euros | Piazza della Signoria 9–10 | www.guccimuseo.com*

8 LOGGIA DEI LANZI ● (130 C5) (*ΩΩ F5*)

With its three majestic round arches, the loggia is a prime example of Florentine Gothic. Cosimo I had two groups of figures erected: the bronze masterpiece *Perseus* (1545–54) by Benvenuto Cellini stands in all its former glory and in its original position (the marble plinth is a copy; the original is in the *Museo Nazionale del Bargello,* see p. 51). The Mannerist work of intertwined figures *The Rape of the Sabines,* to the right, is by Giambologna (1583). Further sculptures, including six statues of Roman women along the rear wall, complete the decorative picture. As early as 1376–82, the city council, the

The most impressive outdoor gallery in the city: the Loggia dei Lanzi at the Piazza della Signoria

Signoria, had the loggia built for receptions and other ceremonial occasions. It is thought by some to have been designed by Orcagna. The name *Loggia dei Lanzi* harks back to the days when Cosimo I's German mercenaries, the *lanzichenecchi* (so-called *Landsknechte*) were stationed here. In 1583, a famous hanging garden was laid out on the roof of the loggia; today it is the site of a ☕ café which is accessible from the Uffizi and from which you have a marvellous view across the piazza. *Piazza della Signoria*

◾9 LOGGIA DEL MERCATO NUOVO (130 C4) (Ⓜ F5)

Rub the snout of a wild boar on the southern side of this covered walkway to ensure your return to Florence. But no fear, the boar is made of bronze and was designed by the sculptor Pietro Tacca who died in Florence in 1540. The loggia of the Mercato Nuovo was built in the same period when this style of covered market had its heyday. Gold and silver were once traded here and later straw items and baskets. Today, the market sells all sorts of tacky goods, mainly scarves and leather goods, to tourists. The best time to appreciate the loggia's architecture is on Sundays and Monday mornings in winter when the stalls have vanished and do not block the view. *Via Porta Rossa/Via Por Santa Maria*

◾10 MUSEO DEL BIGALLO (130 C3) (Ⓜ F5)

On the corner of the Piazza S. Giovanni near the cathedral, lay brethren would let unwanted and orphaned children play underneath their loggia, with the aim of finding parents for them. The *Fratellanza della Misericordia* had commissioned the late Gothic building in 1352. In 1425, the brotherhood united with the Compagnia di Santa Maria del Bigallo, which gave its name to the loggia.

SOUTHERN SAN GIOVANNI

Downstairs is the surgery of the *Misericordia* emergency doctors who offer their services free of charge (see p. 22). The upper floor houses a small, but informative, art exhibition on the activities of the order. *Mon–Sat 10.30am–4.30pm, Sun 9.30am–12.30pm | admission 3 euros | only with reservation: tel. 0 55 28 84 96 | Piazza San Giovanni 1*

⓫ MUSEO SALVATORE FERRAGAMO (130 B4) (*ΩD F5*)

The countless pairs of shoes in the rooms on the lower floors of the Palazzo Spini Feroni tell the story of the footwear maestro Salvatore Ferragamo (1927–60) and the associated brand. They include models worn by such stars as Marilyn Monroe, Greta Garbo, Audrey Hepburn or Judy Garland. Frequent special exhibitions. *Daily 10am–7.30pm | admission 6 euros | Piazza Santa Trinita 5r | www. museoferragamo.it*

⓬ ORSANMICHELE (130 C4) (*ΩD F5*)

A stop-off at the church of Orsanmichele is a must for all Florence visitors. The history of this place of worship, which resembles a medieval palace rather than a church, is typical of the Florentine sense of practicality.

The once open arcades of the ground floor, built in 1336 by the guilds – alongside functioning as a place of worship – served as a market hall and the floors above as a grain store. Around the middle of the 14th century, the arcades of the loggia were closed by means of triple-lancet windows, and Andrea Orcagna erected a monumental Gothic tabernacle around Bernardo Daddi's 1347 painting *Madonna delle Grazie*.

The market was moved in 1361 from the ground floor; the two upper floors were used as a grain store until well into the 16th century. Openings in the northern pillars indicate where, in times of food shortages, the sacks of grain were low-

TIME TO CHILL

Grab yourself a good read and relax in a bar. If this is your idea of an enjoyable, relaxing day, head for somewhere like the *Ibs* **(130 C3)** (*ΩD F4*) *(Mon–Thu 9am–8pm, Fri/Sat until 11pm, Sun 10.30am–8pm | Via de' Cerretani 16r)* or combined with a breakfast *(brunch noon–5pm)*, a vegetarian or even vegan menu at the *Brac* **(131 D5)** (*ΩD G6*) *(Mon–Sat noon–4pm and 7pm–midnight, Sun 6pm–midnight | Via dei Vagellai 18r | tel. 05 50 94 48 77 | www. libreriabrac.net)*.

At the bookshop *Red* **(130 C3)** (*ΩD F3*) *(daily 9am–11pm | Piazza della Repubblica 26/29)*, you can have a bite anytime;

there's WiFi and nice books on art, architecture, design and fashion.

And there is nothing more refreshing than sitting over a cocktail at the *Bar Flò* **(138 B4)** (*ΩD H7*) *(Tue–Sun from 8pm | Piazzale Michelangelo 84 | www. flofirenze.com)* with the most beautiful city in the world at your feet. A wellness package at the spa of the ● *Golden Tower Hotel* **(130 B4)** (*ΩD F5*) *(reserve in advance! | Piazza Strozzi 11r | tel. 0 55 28 78 60)* gets you going again. Enjoy the elegant surroundings of ● *SoulSpace (daily 10am–8pm | Via Sant'Egidio 12 | tel. 05 52 00 17 94)* with pool, hamam and great treatments.

Step back in time to see how rich Florentines lived 500 years ago at the Palazzo Davanzati

ered down to be distributed free of charge to the needy – in the hope of warding off possible unrest. Today, the upper floors are used to stage exhibitions – a good opportunity to take a look at the fine Gothic rooms. Statues of the patron saints of the guilds, fashioned by the most important Renaissance sculptors, stand in 14 niches on the exterior. Most of the statues, including Donatello's famous *marble statue of St George*, patron saint of armourers, have been replaced with bronze replicas. The originals are now in the *Museo Nazionale del Bargello* (see p. 51). *Mon–Fri 10am–5pm, Sat 10am–12.30pm | free admission | Via dell'Arte della Lana*

13 INSIDER TIP PALAZZO DAVANZATI
(130 B4) (*M F5*)

Discover one of the finest palaces in the city: complete with furniture, paintings and other objects, it gives a true reflection of Florentine houses between the Middle Ages and the Renaissance. The brilliance of the magnificent murals in the *Sala dei Papagalli* (Parrot Room) as well as in the gentlemen's and ladies' chambers has recently been painstakingly restored. Bedrooms and kitchen on the 2nd and 3rd floors can only be visited at 10am, 11am and noon by appointment *(tel. 05 52 38 86 10). Daily 8.15am–1.50pm, closed 2nd and 4th Sun as well as 1st, 3rd and 5th Mon in the month | admission 6 euros | Via Porta Rossa 13*

14 PALAZZO STROZZI ●
(130 B4) (*M F5*)

The epitome of the Florentine Renaissance palace. No fewer than 15 houses had to be demolished in order to build this structure of roughly hewn stone on this prominent site. Construction began in 1489 under Benedetto da Maiano and was completed in 1536 by Simone del Pollaiuolo, "il Cronaca". He was also responsible for the generously proportioned, arcaded inner courtyards. Today, the palazzo stages art exhibitions. *Fri–Wed 10am–8pm, Thu until 11pm | admission 12 euros | Piazza Strozzi | www.palazzostrozzi.org*

15 PALAZZO VECCHIO ★ ⋋⋌
(131 D5) *(ᴍ F5)*

This splendid, crenellated palace with its 94-m (308 ft)-high tower was built between 1299 and 1314 by Arnolfo di Cambio and served initially as the seat of government and living quarters of the highest officials in the Republic.

In 1540, Cosimo I turned the medieval palace into his ducal residence. The additions and conversions he had carried out created a dazzling interior, while the medieval exterior remained largely unchanged. Giorgio Vasari was charged with overseeing the building work, though his heightened enthusiasm for the task led him to overlay certain irreplaceable works, such as Leonardo da Vinci's *Battle of Ang-*

hiari in the Salone dei Cinquecento, with his own paintings illustrating the fame and fortune of the Medicis. The palace took on its current name, *Palazzo Vecchio* (Old Palace), when the ducal court moved to the "new" one, the Palazzo Pitti.

The beautiful *inner courtyard,* modified in 1470 by Michelozzo, was decorated with frescoes depicting Austrian cityscapes to mark the wedding of Ferdinand I and Johanna of Austria in 1565. The *Quartieri Monumentali*, the magnificent private apartments, are on the 1st floor.

The huge *Salone dei Cinquecento*, the Room of the Five Hundred, was originally the debating hall of the municipal council and was later converted into an audience chamber by Cosimo I. The 53.7-m-long, 22.4-m-wide and 17.8-m-high chamber (58.7yd x 25.5yd x 19.5yd) is the largest room in the city and – like the *Sala dei Dugento* also crowned by a fabulously

Filigree Renaissance grotesques and city scenes adorn the Palazzo Vecchio courtyard

carved wooden ceiling by Michelozzo – is still used on festive occasions. Marble statues, among them the *Genius of Victory* by Michelangelo and *Florence defeating Pisa* by Giambologna, stand in front of Vasari's monumental battle scenes.

On the 2nd floor are the *Quartieri degli Elementi* and the apartments of Eleonora di Toledo, wife of Cosimo I. The adjacent *Cappella della Signoria* was ornamented with frescoes by Ghirlandaio in 1514. The *Sala dell'Udienza* is particularly impressive, with its elaborately carved ceiling and the marble doorway by Benedetto da Maiano, as is the *Sala dei Gigli*, decorated entirely with the French emblem, the *fleur-de-lys*. Here stands Donatello's bronze composition *Judith and Holofernes*. As Secretary to the Second Chancery of the Republic, Niccoló Machiavelli worked in the *Segreteria*. The *Guardaroba*, the "Wardrobe Room", contains cupboards painted with 53 maps from the period 1563–75. The oldest part of the palace, the former armoury *(Sala d'Arme)*, today stages changing exhibitions. The entrance is on the left-hand side of the palace.

Twelve multimedia stations give you an insight into the history, art and architecture of the building. A bookshop and the ticket office have been re-located to the second inner courtyard, the *Cortile della Dogana*. The entrance to the *Museo dei Ragazzi*, an excellent museum for children (and their parents), is also accessed from here. Furthermore, it is possible to take a look at previously inaccessible parts of the palace in guided tours of the so-called INSIDER TIP secret passages *(percorsi segreti)*. *Palace/Museum/Quartieri Monumentali: April–Sept Fri–Wed 9am–11pm, Thu 9am–2pm, Oct–March Fri–Wed 9am–7pm, Thu 9am–2pm; tower: Fri–Wed 10am–5pm, Thu 10am–2pm, closed when it rains | admission 10 euros | Percorsi segreti and Museo dei Ragazzi: appointment by phone; Mon–Sat 9.30am–5pm, Sun until 12.30pm | supplementary charge: 2 euros | tel. 05 52 76 83 25 | Piazza della Signoria | entry via the Via dei Gondi | museivicifiorentini.comune.fi.it*

16 PIAZZA DELLA SIGNORIA
(130 C4–5) *(m F5)*

Dominated by the fortress-like Palazzo Vecchio, the square is simply breathtaking. The *Loggia dei Lanzi* with its statues and the *Uffizi* Galleries form the southern boundary of the piazza, on the north side is the *Palazzo Uguccioni* (1559) and on the bulging eastern flank stands the *Tribunale della Mercanzia* (Tribunal of Merchandise, 1359), whose façade is adorned with the coats of arms of the 21 guilds. The buildings opposite the palace, which house cafés and shops, were built at the end of the 19th century in a style echoing their surroundings.

The many statues and monuments scattered across the square serve to give it a pleasant, more informal atmosphere. Highlights in front of the Palazzo Vecchio include the gigantic marble figure of *David* by Michelangelo (1504, a copy; the original is in the Galleria dell'Accademia); the group *Hercules and Caco* by Baccio Bandinelli (1533) and Donatello's 1460 bronze composition *Judith and Holofernes* (copy; original in the Palazzo Vecchio).

Between the imposing *Fontana de Nettuno* (Neptune Fountain) by Bartolomeo Ammanati (1565) and Giambologna's bronze *equestrian statue of Cosimo I de' Medici* (1594), a granite slab inscribed with the date 1498 is set into the ground. It marks the spot where Dominican monk Girolamo Savonarola and two of his supporters were burnt at the stake by order of the Borgia Pope Alexander VI. Every year on 23 May, the anniversary of the execution, representatives of the Church and the city lay a floral tribute here.

17 PONTE SANTA TRÍNITA ✂
(130 B5) (*F5*)

The bridge was swept away by floods on the Arno River several times before eventually being destroyed by retreating German troops in 1944. When reconstruction began, its remnants were fished out of the river, and the quarries in the Boboli Gardens, from which the original stone came, were opened again to source material for its repair. From here, you have a sensational view upstream to the Ponte Vecchio, particularly memorable at sunset.

it was where most of the city's butchers plied their trade. When the ducal family moved to the Palazzo Pitti, they were disturbed by the stench, and Ferdinand I decreed that, from then onwards, only gold and silversmiths could conduct their business on the bridge. Since he wanted to be able to get from the Palazzo Vecchio to the Palazzo Pitti without getting his feet wet, Cosimo I commissioned Giorgio Vasari in 1565 with the building of the *Corridoio Vasariano*, which runs above the shops on the eastern side. The

A narrow river bank setting on the Arno invites guests to chill out in the evening

18 PONTE VECCHIO ★ ● ✂
(130 B–C5) (*F5*)

The "Old Bridge" is one of the landmarks of Florence. Even back in Etruscan times there was a river crossing point here, and Via Cassia, one of the most important Roman trade routes, led northwards along this way. The bridge, which crosses the river at its narrowest point, was built in 1345 by Neri di Fioravanti or Taddeo Gaddi. It is characterised by the overhanging construction of the shops which line the bridge. From 1422 to 1593

Ponte Vecchio was the only bridge not blown up by the German army in 1944; to spare the bridge, however, large sections of the old residential areas on either side of it were destroyed. Today, the bridge and its jeweller's boutiques is a major crowd-puller in the city.

19 SANTISSIMI APOSTOLI
(130 B5) (*F5*)

The Church of the Holy Apostles (11th century) is a beautiful small parish church, set back somewhat from the well-trodden tourist routes. It was built in the form of an Early Christian basilica with a semi-circular apse. According to a plaque on the façade, the church was a donation of Charlemagne, though this subsequently turned out to be a myth. Some of the black-green marble columns of the interior originate from nearby Roman thermal baths. The painted roof timbering (14th century) is the best preserved of its kind in the city. A narrow passageway leads from the square in front of the church through the houses of the Lungarno Corsini down to the river. *Tue–Fri 4pm–7pm | Piazza del Limbo 1*

NORTHERN SAN GIOVANNI

The district to the north of the cathedral is split into two distinct areas: one surrounds the Basilica di San Lorenzo, with the large market hall of the same name and colourful stalls outside it; the other stretches from the Piazza del Duomo to San Marco and Santissima Annunziata, where the university of Florence was once situated. Most faculties have since been relocated to Novoli, and with them, many students have also left the area.

Only the art students at the famous *Accademia di Belle Arti,* under the arcades of the busy Piazza San Marco, make for a student atmosphere. Yet northern San Giovanni has undergone even more changes in the last few years. The presence of many immigrants – whether they be recent arrivals in the city or second- or third-generation residents – has turned this into a multicultural but also rather down-at-heel district – depending on which way you look at things. Although the city's main attractions are centred in San Giovanni, here in the streets to the north of the

duomo, you no longer have the feeling of being surrounded only by tourists.

■ BIBLIOTECA MEDICEA LAURENZIANA (130 C2) (*ℳ F4*)

The library, which was completed in 1578, contains one of the most valuable collections of manuscripts in the world. Michelangelo designed the architecturally most unconventional vestibule, with its grandiose INSIDER TIP *staircase,* as well as the INSIDER TIP *Sala Grande* (Main Reading Room) opening out from it, the lecterns and the wooden ceiling. The pattern of the ceiling is taken up by the floor. *Mon, Wed, Fri 8am–2pm, Tue, Thu 8am–5.30pm | admission 3 euros | Piazza San Lorenzo 9 | entry to the left of the church façade | www.bmlonline.it*

■ GALLERIA DELL'ACCADEMIA ★ (131 D–E1) (*ℳ G4*)

Little has changed in the halls and corridors of the Accademia di Belle Arti since the days when Michelangelo Buonarroti (1475–1564) sculpted his works here. He, on the other hand, maybe would be surprised to see the hordes of tourists who come to the Galleria next door (founded in 1784 by the merger of the Ospedale San Matteo with the adjoining monastery) to admire some of his major works.

One of his works overshadows the rest, however; *David.* Magnificently hewn from a single 6-tonne block of white Carrara marble, this 4.10 m/13 ft-high sculpture simply takes your breath away. Along the walls of the main exhibition room stand the unfinished marble sculptures of the four *Prisoners* as well as a statue of *St. Matthew,* originally destined for the city's cathedral. Michelangelo's *Pietà of Palestrina* is also stunningly beautiful as well as the largest European collection of late *Gothic paint-*

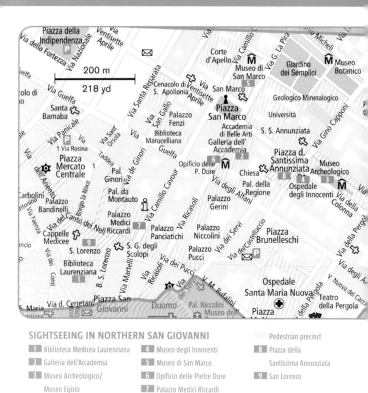

SIGHTSEEING IN NORTHERN SAN GIOVANNI

1 Biblioteca Medicea Laurenziana
2 Galleria dell'Accademia
3 Museo Archeologico/ Museo Egizio
4 Museo degli Innocenti
5 Museo di San Marco
6 Opificio delle Pietre Dure
7 Palazzo Medici Riccardi
8 Piazza della Santissima Annunziata
9 San Lorenzo

Pedestrian precinct

ings and other works by Italian artists of the 13th to 15th centuries on display in the adjoining rooms. Last but not least, don't miss the refectory full of *stucco statues*. *Tue–Sun 8.15am–6.50pm | admission 8 euros, special exhibitions 12.50 euros, advance booking, tel. 0 55 29 48 83 (supplementary charge: 4 euros) | Via Ricasoli 60 | www.galleriaaccademiafirenze.beni culturali.it*

3 MUSEO ARCHEOLOGICO/ MUSEO EGIZIO (131 F1–2) (*⌖ G4*)
Besides the fearsome *Chimaere of Arezzo* dating back to the 4th century BC, the museum houses other bizarre artefacts.

The Archaeological Museum houses the most impressive collection of Etruscan treasures outside the Villa Giulia in Rome and also the second-largest Egyptian collection, after Turin. Besides Etruscan and Egyptian objects, there are also prehistoric, Greek and Roman finds on display, for example the famous *François Vase* decorated in the black-figure style with scenes from Greek mythology (600 BC). The beautiful garden contains restored Etruscan tombstones. *Tue–Fri 8.30am–7pm, Sat–Mon until 2pm; closed 2nd, 4th and 5th Sun of the month | admission 4 euros | Piazza della Santissima Annunziata 9b | www.polomusealetoscana.beniculturali.it*

4 MUSEO DEGLI INNOCENTI ●
(131 E1) (*m G4*)

Since 1445, unwanted newborn babies have been left at the hospital by pushing them through a revolving door in the narrow loggia wall on the left. The museum belongs to the *Spedale degli Innocenti* (Hospital of the Innocent) and was opened in 2016. On exhibition in the large crypt are the highly emotive stories of 140 of the more than 1000 foundlings who were accepted by the hospital between the middle of the 15th century and 1875. In the basement, sound installations and photos are used to trace the

have seen over a cappuccino and take in the fab views over Florence. *Admission 10 euros | Piazza della Santissima Annunziata 12*

5 MUSEO DI SAN MARCO
(134 A5) (*m G3*)

Despite being an austere monk, he was also devoted to the brightest colours. When Cosimo I endowed the monks of San Domenico in Fiesole with a monastery in the city in 1435, they gave their fellow Dominican, Fra Angelico, the task of decorating it. The colourful frescoes with which the monk filled the cells, the

The monk as painter: Fra Angelico painted the San Marco monastery for his friars

hospital's fascinating architectural history while the halls on the first floor show a small yet sensational collection of frescoes and artworks, which include the magnificent Adorazione dei Magi degli Innocenti (1485) by Domenico Ghirlandaio. The stunning, ☆ INSIDER TIP partly covered rooftop café terrace is the perfect place to contemplate on what you

refectory and even the monastery corridors over a period of ten years (1435–45) earned him the name *Beato* ("the blessed one") even during his lifetime. Fra Angelico's large fresco in the Chapter House showing the *Crucifixion,* a *Last Supper* fresco by Domenico Ghirlandaio in the small refectory and, at the head of the staircase to the cell tract, Fra Angelico's most famous work, *The Annunciation,* are highly deserving of a closer look.

Each of the 43 cells was adorned with a fresco by Fra Angelico or one of his assistants. Cells 12 to 14, which were for the Prior's use, now serve as a memorial to Girolamo Savonarola. Cosimo de' Medici often retreated to the double cell 38/39 for extended periods of meditation. Also on the upper floor, the well proportioned *library* by Michelozzo (1444) contains 115 precious codices, miniatures, manuscripts and an illuminated prayer book by Fra Angelico. *Mon–Fri 8.15am–1.50pm, Sat/Sun until 4.50pm, closed 1st, 3rd and 5th Sun as well as 2nd and 4th Mon in the month | admission 4 euros | Piazza di San Marco 1 | www.polomusealitoscana.beniculturali.it*

6 OPIFICIO DELLE PIETRE DURE (131 D1) (*map* G4)

In this world-famous academy for restoration work, craftsmen still fashion the mosaics out of semi-precious stones and marble for which Florence has been famous since the Renaissance. The finest examples of this *pietra dure* technique are to be seen in the *Cappella dei Principi* in San Lorenzo. Here, the original designs and a model of the chapel as well as countless other works are on display. *Mon–Sat 8.15am–2pm | admission 4 euros | Via degli Alfani 78 | www.opificio dellepietredure.it*

7 PALAZZO MEDICI RICCARDI (130 C2) (*map* F4)

Cosimo the Elder lived here with his family until his death in 1464. Twenty years previously he had engaged Michelozzo to build this prestigious palace which has a grand, rusticated façade. The inner courtyard and arcades, crowned by the Medici coat of arms, were a particular innovation. The *Cappella dei Magi,* decorated by Benozzo Gozzoli in 1459 with delightful landscape frescos, and a few of the rooms on the 1st floor are open to the public. The other rooms house the provincial administration of Florence. *Thu–Tue 9am–5pm | admission 7 euros | Via Camillo Cavour 1*

8 PIAZZA DELLA SANTISSIMA ANNUNZIATA (131 E1) (*map* G4)

You can tell by the smell of tasty *frittelle* wafting over the square: on 25 March every year, the square hosts the Feast of the Annunciation, as did the farmers on the day when they once brought their local produce to sell in the city. This feast recalls that, until 1749 when the Archduke finally issued a decree that the Gregorian calendar was to be adopted, the stubborn Florentines celebrated New Year on 25 March, the day of the Virgin Mary's Annunciation, precisely nine months to the day before the birth of Christ. The miraculous image of the

FIT IN THE CITY

If you want to go for a jog, take the bus (12, 13, 17 and 18) to the *Parco delle Cascine:* the over 3 km (1.86 miles) of pathways along the Arno are ideal for running, while the rollerbladers get together on the asphalted avenues which criss-cross the 118-ha (1 mi²) park. *Sight jogging* combines fitness with taking in the sights. To do this, you can get yourself a personal trainer for 45–80 euros per person – depending on the route and how long you want to go for, e.g. via *Go Running Tours (www.gorunningtours. com)* or at the *Hotel River* (138 B3) (*map* H6) *(Tel. 05 52 34 35 29 | www. hotelriver.com)*

Virgin Mary – the largest treasure of the *Santissima Annunziata* church (in the chapel immediately to the left of the nave), which, according to legend, was completed by an angel one night in 1252 – is only revealed on 25 March every year. The *cloisters (daily 7.30am–12.30pm and 4pm–6.30pm)* show paintings by Rosso Fiorentino, Pontormo and Andrea del Sarto and the frescoes by Andrea del Castagno and Perugino in the side chapels are worth a closer look.

The harmonious *square*, featuring an equestrian statue of Ferdinand I by Giambologna and two whimsical fountains by Pietro Tacca, is surrounded on three sides by elegant porticos. The buildings were originally constructed to accommodate sleeping for pilgrims coming to venerate the Virgin Mary, but were later extended. In 1419, Filippo Brunelleschi began building the *Spedale degli Innocenti*, a foundling hospital. Look up to admire the portico decorated by Andrea della Robbia with terracotta medallions of babies in swaddling clothes which line the western side of the square. Opposite this is the *Loggia di Servi di Maria* built by Antonio da Sangallo from 1516–25.

The loneliness of a long-distance runner? A rare sight in Florence

9 SAN LORENZO ★ (130 C2) (𝄞 F4)

There is not one single stone in this church which is not linked in some way to a member of the Medici family. Giovanni di Bicci, patriarch of the dynasty, commissioned Brunelleschi in around 1420 with the extension of an Early Christian place of worship, consecrated in the name of St Lawrence back in 393 AD. First, Brunelleschi completed the *Sagrestia Vecchia* (Old Sacristy) in 1428, the first central-plan building of the Renaissance. Cosimo the Elder, Giovanni's son, continued with construction of the church after his death until its comple-

tion in 1446. He lies buried in the crypt. A colourful, round stone slab in front of the main altar indicates the position of the grave. Donatello also found his last resting place alongside his friend and sponsor, Cosimo il Vecchio.

Pope Leo X, Cosimo's great-grandson, made a decisive contribution to the transformation of the church complex into a giant mausoleum, the INSIDER TIP *Cappelle Medicee (daily 8.15am–6pm, closed 2nd, 4th Sun and 1st, 3rd and 5th Mon in the month | admission 8 euros, special exhibitions 9 euros | access: Piazza Madonna degli*

Aldobrandini 6 | www.cappellemedicee. it) when he engaged Michelangelo to build the *Sagrestia Nuova* (New Sacristy). It contains the remarkable tombs of Lorenzo il Magnifico, his brother Giuliano and their descendants Giuliano, Duke of Nemours, as well as Lorenzo, Duke of Urbino – each of them the work of Michelangelo. At the beginning of the 17th century, the construction of the *Cappella dei Principi* (Chapel of the Princes), its interior entirely adorned with semiprecious stones, marked the completion of the veneration of the ruling family.

A door on the left of the church leads to the cloisters and the *Biblioteca Medicea Laurenziana.* Tenders were invited for the design of the original rough-cut stone façade we still see today, and plans by Michelangelo do actually exist but were never realised. *Mon–Sat 10am– 5pm, March–Oct also Sun 1.30pm–5pm |*

admission 3.50 euros | Piazza di San Lorenzo | www.operamedicealaurenziana. org

SANTA MARIA NOVELLA

One of the city's most beautiful churches, with its splendid marble façade, lends a district and the square in front its name: *Santa Maria Novella.*

The district stretches from the main railway station of the same name northwards as far as the *Fortezza da Basso* and westwards to the 1.6 km^2/0.62 square mile *Parco delle Cascine* – the only public green space in the city. To the south, it is bordered by the River Arno and the luxury shopping street *Via dei Tornabuoni*.

The luxury shopping mile Via dei Tornabuoni is just a few steps away from the Museo Marino Marini

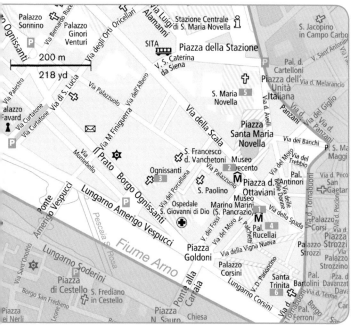

SIGHTSEEING IN SANTA MARIA NOVELLA

Pedestrian precinct

1 Museo Marino Marini
2 Museo Novecento
3 Ognissanti
4 Palazzo Rucellai
5 Santa Maria Novella
6 Santa Trinita

1 MUSEO MARINO MARINI
(130 A–B3) (∅ E–F5)

Since 1988, the former church of San Pancrazio, which dates back to the Early Christian period, has housed the city's first museum dedicated to modern art. **INSIDER TIP** Over 200 representations of horses by the sculptor, painter and graphic artist Marino Marini (1901–80) from nearby Pistoia are on display in this skilfully converted place of worship.

The museum was extended in 2013 to include a different type of sacred architectural treasure: a tiny chapel that had been hidden away since Napoleon's time. Following extensive renovation, you can once again enter the splendid **INSIDER TIP** *Sacello Rucellai* and admire the tomb which Giovanni Rucellai had made for himself by Leon Battista Alberti around 1570. *Wed–Fri 10am–1pm, Sat–Mon 10am–7pm | admission 6 euros | Piazza di San Pancrazio | www.museomarinomarini.it*

2 **INSIDER TIP** MUSEO NOVECENTO
(130 A3) (∅ E4)

The city of Florence is proud owner of over 300 masterpieces from 20th century Italian painters that had, until 2014, never been exhibited before. Visitors can now admire works from Giorgio de Chirico, Carlo Carrà, Gorgio Morandi and Marino Marini spread over 15 exhibition rooms in the new 800 m² five-floor museum. *April–Sept Sat–Wed 11am–8pm, Thu until 2pm, Fri until 11pm, Oct–March Fri–Wed 11am–7pm, Thu until 2pm | admission 8.50 euros | Piazza Santa Maria Novella 10 | www.museonovecento.it*

3 OGNISSANTI (133 D6) *(ᗡ E5)*

The All Saints' Church is a typical example of a sacred building which has been sponsored by a powerful family. The Vespucci's generous patronage not only paid for much of the furnishings of the church, but also founded the adjacent *San Giovanni di Dio* hospital in 1380, which continued in this function until recently.

The second church altar on the right features an early work by Ghirlandaio from around 1473: the Virgin Mary spreads her cloak protectively over the members of the Vespucci family. The young man below her right arm is presumed to be the seafarer Amerigo Vespucci, who gave his name to the newly discovered continent of America. In the second chapel of the right transept a round stone slab marks the burial place of the great Florentine painter of the early Renaissance, Sandro Botticelli, who was also responsible for the fresco of St Augustine in the monastery refectory. After ten years of restoration work, Giotto's famous INSIDER TIP *Crucifix* from the 14th century can once again be marvelled at in the left transept. In the same room, you should also take a look at the large *Cenacolo del Ghirlandaio,* Ghirlandaio's fresco depicting the *Last Supper* (1480). *Thu–Tue 9.30am–12.30pm, 4pm–7.30pm, Wed 4pm–7.30pm | free admission | Borgo Ognissanti 42 | www.chiesaognissanti.it*

4 PALAZZO RUCELLAI (130 A–B4) *(ᗡ E5)*

Built in 1451, this Renaissance palace belonging to the rich merchant Giovanni Rucellai rates as the most elegant in the city. It epitomises the credo of builder and architect Leon Battista Alberti (1402–72) that palatial residences should be "beautifully ornamented, elegant and clearly proportioned, rather than ostentatious and imposing". The Rucellai family still live in the palace to this day, which means that the interior is not open to the public. *Via della Vigna Nuova 16*

5 SANTA MARIA NOVELLA (130 A2) *(ᗡ E4)*

In the first story of the *Decameron,* we read of "... the venerable church of Santa Maria Novella..." Boccaccio's tale is set during the plague which ravaged 14th-century Florence. The survivors founded numerous chapels in the church to express their gratitude. This first Gothic building in the city was begun in 1246 and finished in 1300. The outer walls are clad in white and green marble, in the style of the Battistero. The upper section of the façade, however, was only completed in 1470 thanks to the sponsorship of the Florentine merchant Giovanni Rucellai.

It is worth taking your time to examine the interior, too. The large cycles of frescoes give an insight into residential styles and fashions of the 15th century. Among the most beautiful are those by Domenico Ghirlandaio in the choir (1486–90), depicting scenes from the life of the Virgin Mary, the frescoes in the *Cappella Strozzi* to the right of the main altar by Filippino Lippi and the bleak visions of *The Last Judgement* by Nardo di Cione (around 1357) in the *Cappella Strozzi di Mantova.* In the left of the nave, Masaccio's *Trinity,* painted shortly before his death in 1428, demonstrates a revolutionary awareness

The tiny Santa Trinita church with fantastic frescoes is a frequently overlooked beauty

and realisation of perspective and proportion. The church also contains works by Brunelleschi (the marble pulpit and a wooden Crucifix in the *Cappella Gondi*, to the left of the main altar), Giotto (Crucifix) and Giovanni della Robbia.

Don't miss the neighbouring *Chiostro verde* (Green Cloister) from 1332, ornamented by Paolo Uccello with images from the Creation story (sadly in poor condition), and the *Cappella Spagnola* (Spanish Chapel) with frescoes showing the *Triumphant Dominican Order* by Andrea da Firenze. *Mon–Thu 9am–5.30pm, Fri 11am–5.30pm, Sat 9am–5pm, Sun July–Sept noon–5pm, Oct–June 1pm–5pm | admission 7.50 euros | Piazza di Santa Maria Novella 18 | www.smn.it*

6 INSIDER TIP SANTA TRÍNITA
(130 B4) (ꭥ F5)

The church with its origins in the second half of the 11th century has among its many art treasures two major works by Domenico Ghirlandaio: the frescoes in the *Cappella Sassetti* from the life of St Francis and the *Adoration of the Magi* from 1485. *Daily 7am–noon and 4pm–7pm | Piazza Santa Trínita*

SANTA CROCE

It's the liveliest quarter in Florence: many small shops are an invitation to shop, and the restaurants around the Franciscan church Santa Croce serve up not only the finest the Tuscan kitchen has to offer, but also the whole spectrum of international cuisine.

As far back as Roman times, this quarter was dedicated to entertainment. The 2nd-century *amphitheatre* stood facing the western end of the square – as indicated today by the curvature of the roads around the Piazza de' Peruzzi, Via Bentaccordi and Via Torta. At the southern end of the piazza, below the fresco-

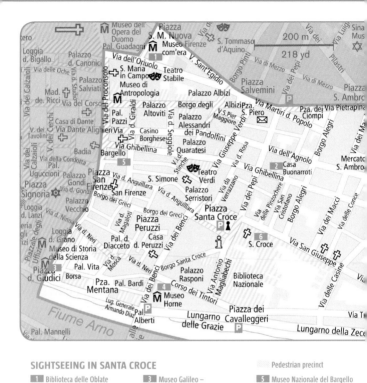

SIGHTSEEING IN SANTA CROCE

1 Biblioteca delle Oblate
2 Casa Buonarroti
3 Museo Galileo – Istituto di Storia della Scienza
4 Museo Horne
5 Museo Nazionale del Bargello
6 Santa Croce

Pedestrian precinct

covered façade of the *Palazzo dell'Antella*, you'll spot a marble disc set into the wall. This marks the halfway line of the "field" on which *Calcio in Costume* is played (see p. 23) – which makes this piazza one of the oldest football pitches in the world!

1 BIBLIOTECA DELLE OBLATE ●
(131 E3) (Ⓜ G5)

The former 14th-century monastery, with its fine cloisters, now houses the municipal library and a media archive *(Wed 9am–2pm, Thu/Fri 9am–5pm)*. You should visit the ☃ INSIDER TIP roof ter-

race with its sensational close-up view of the dome of the cathedral. Or take a break with an international newspaper at the *Caffetteria* among all the students. *Mon 2pm–10pm, Tue–Fri 9am–midnight, Sat 10am–midnight | Via dell'Oriuolo 26*

2 CASA BUONARROTI
(131 F4) (Ⓜ G6)

This small palazzo was bought by Michelangelo and presented as a gift to the city by a descendent, Cosimo Buonarroti, in 1858. Drawings, plans and mementos of the great artist are on display. Among the early works are the famous marble reliefs *Madonna della Scala* (Madonna of the Stairs) and the *Battle of the Centaurs*. *Nov–Feb Wed–Mon 10am–4.30pm, March–Oct Wed–Mon 10am–5pm | admission 6.50 euros | Via Ghibellina 70 | www.casabuonarroti.it*

③ INSIDER TIP MUSEO GALILEO – ISTITUTO DI STORIA DELLA SCIENZA (130 C5) (*GU F5*)

The museum is one of the most important of its kind in the world. A large part of it is dedicated to Galileo Galilei. In nine large rooms, mathematic, optical, hydraulic, astronomic and surgical devices are on show, including models of the planets, the first telescope and mercury thermometer (1634) and a fine collection of minerals. Don't miss the telescope and lenses the illustrious astronomer used to make his observations and through which he discovered Jupiter's moons, for example. *Wed–Mon 9.30am–6pm, Tue until 1pm | admission 9 euros | Piazza dei Giudici 1 | www.museogalileo.it*

④ MUSEO HORNE (131 E5) (*GU G6*)

When English art historian and architect Herbert Percy Horne died in 1916, he bequeathed the 15th-century *Palazzo Corsi*, purchased in 1911, to the Italian state. The donation also includes his sizeable art collection of over 6,000 works by artists such as Giotto, Simone Martini, Filippo Lippi, Masaccio and Giambologna as well as precious items of furniture from the 14th to 16th centuries. *Mon–Sat 9am–1pm, winter Thu–Tue 10am–2pm | admission 7 euros | Via dei Benci 6 | www.museohorne.it*

⑤ MUSEO NAZIONALE DEL BARGELLO ★ ● (131 D4) (*GU G5*)

Behind the crenellated façade of the Bargello you will find the largest collection of Italian sculptures from the 14th to 16th centuries, the Medici medal collection, significant ivory pieces and majolica from the 15th to 18th centuries, weapons and small bronze objects. Museum highlights are Michelangelo's *Bacchus* (begun in 1497), the marble bust of *Brutus* (around 1540) and the circular *Tondo Pitti* (1504), which are on

Museo Nazionale del Bargello: the Baptistry on a wedding chest

SANTA CROCE

show on the ground floor together with works by Cellini, Giambologna and others. The main room on the upper floor contains Early Renaissance sculptures, including Donatello's *David statues* in marble (1408) and in bronze (1423).

Crowned by a 54-m-high (178 ft) tower, the fortress-like palace itself was built in 1254–61 and served as the headquarters of the *Capitano del Popolo* (military governor) and the *podestà* (mayor). From 1502 to 1859, this was the city prison and residence of the *bargello* (captain of police), after whom the building is now named. The gallows – in use until 1782 – stood next to the fountain in the pretty courtyard decorated with coats of arms. *Daily 8.15am– 4:30pm, closed 2nd and 4th Mon; 1st, 3rd and 5th Sun of the month; special exhibitions Mon–Fri 8.15am–1.50pm, Sat/Sun until 4.50pm | admission 8 euros, special exhibitions: 9 euros | Via dell'Arte della Lana | www.bargellomu sei.beniculturali.it*

6 SANTA CROCE ★
(131 E–F5) (*øʊ G5*)

Santa Croce is the main Franciscan church in Florence. Shortly after his death in 1226, followers of St Francis erected a small chapel here. Soon it was no longer able to accommodate the number of worshippers, so that the foundation stone for this mighty Gothic building was laid in 1294. It was completed in 1385, and a neo-Gothic façade added in 1853. The basilica is 115 m (125yd) long, the nave 38m (42yd) and the transept 73 m (80yd) wide. Consequently, Santa Croce was larger than the church of the rival Dominican Order, Santa Maria Novella, which had been completed shortly before.

The interior features an open, painted trussed roof and straight choir screen, typical of the unpretentious architecture of the mendicant orders. The church is also known as the "Pantheon of Florence": 278 *memorial slabs* from the 14th to 19th centuries are set into the

floor. Galileo, Michelangelo, Machiavelli, Ghiberti, the composer Rossini and many others are commemorated here with magnificently crafted tombs. Italy's supreme poet, Dante, who died in exile in Ravenna, is also remembered here with a memorial created 500 years after his death. Between 1316 and 1330, Giotto decorated the *funerary chapels of the Bardi and Peruzzi* to the right of the main altar. These frescos are considered to be among the finest of the period. The murals in the other chapels are also outstanding. The magnificent *marble pulpit* is by Benedetto da Maiano and the *Annunciation,* fashioned from gilded grey sandstone, (behind the fifth pillar on the right) is one of Donatello's principle works (1435).

To the right of the church is the entrance to the cloistered courtyards with the *Cappella dei Pazzi* and the *Museo dell'Opera di Santa Croce.* The architecture of the Capella dei Pazzi is notable for its clear forms in white and grey and was prob-ably built by Brunelleschi (1429–44). The glazed terracotta *medallions* are the work of Luca della Robbia. The church museum contains Florentine religious art. *Church and museum: Mon–Sat 9.30am–5pm, Sun 2pm–5pm | admission 8 euros | Piazza di Santa Croce 16 | www.santacroceopera.it*

OLTRARNO

In the district of craftsmen, Oltrarno (beyond the Arno), you can still sense the "old" Florence. Twisting alleyways lead to tiny squares where time stands still in the daytime and which, in the evening, become the backdrop for a mass of young revellers thronging the bars and trattorias.

The charm of the hidden workshops is quite unique – where skilled artisans transform leather, glass, bronze, wood, marble, straw, gold or silver following centuries-old techniques. Oltrarno also

Santa Croce: Built originally for Mendicant orders, the church features notable tombs and cenotaphs

boasts fine Renaissance palaces with antique dealers as well as the grandiose *Palazzo Pitti* and the *Boboli Gardens*.

■1 INSIDER TIP FORTE DI BELVEDERE
⩊⩊ (137 E4) (*ffl F6*)

When Ferdinand I de' Medici commissioned architect Buontalenti in 1590 with the building of this fortress above Florence, he had the cannons trained on the city: the Medici were never really sure of their hold on authority. Inside the fortress is the elegant, three-storey *Palazzetto di Belvedere.* In the wake of two fatal accidents, in which visitors fell from the perimeter wall, the fortress only opens its doors for open air exhibitions. Don't miss them! *Changing opening hours, in the summer mostly 10.30am–7.30pm | admission 3 euros | Via San Leonardo | www.museivicifiorentini.comune.fi.it/fortebelvedere*

■2 GIARDINO DI BOBOLI ★ ● ⩊⩊
(137 D–E4) (*ffl E–F 6–7*)

These splendid gardens extend behind the Palazzo Pitti towards the Porta Romana and up to the Forte di Belvedere and feature tree-lined arcades, cypress avenues, fountains and pools, staircases and artificial grottos, an amphitheatre and hundreds of marble statues. You should set aside three hours for a stroll around the park (45,000 m²/53,820yd²), savouring the fine views of the city. Chamber music concerts on summer evenings. *Daily Nov–Feb 8.15am–4.30pm, March until 5.30pm, April/May and Sept/Oct until 6.30pm, June–Aug until 7.30pm, closed 1st and last Mon in the month | admission 10 euros | entrances Palazzo Pitti, Via Romana and Porta Romana | www.uffizi.it/giardino-boboli*

Giardino di Boboli: the former private gardens of the Medici family are now open to the public

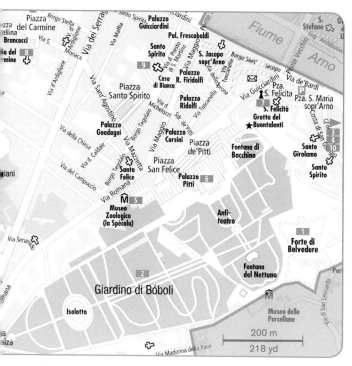

3 GIARDINO & VILLA BARDINI ●
(137 F–64) (*ɯ F6*)

The enchanting gardens of the Villa Bardini offer splendid views over the city. When the wisteria, roses and hydrangeas are in full bloom, you will be escorted up the Baroque open staircase to the Rondò Belvedere by the delightful smells. Dating back to 1641, the villa is home to the fashion designer *Roberto Capucci's* Foundation Museum *(Tue–Sun 10am–7pm | admission 8 euros | www.* fondazionerobertocapucci.com) and the *Museo Pietro Annigoni (Tue–Sun 10am–7pm | admission 8 euros | www.museo-annigoni.it)* of the painter who died in 1988. *Tue–Sun 10am–7pm | admission 8 euros | Costa di San Giorgio 2 | www. bardinipeyron.it*

4 MUSEO STEFANO BARDINI
(138 A4) (*ɯ G6*)

The museum bears the name of the renowned merchant, collector, art restorer and photographer Stefano Bardini (1836–1922), who bequeathed his entire collection of antiques to the city upon his death. Apart from works by artists such as Donatello, Antonio del Pollaiuolo and Tiepolo and many others you can marvel at the original bronze sculpture of the *porcellino* by Pietro Tacca, a replica of which stands in front of the *Loggia del Mercato Nuovo,* much to the delight of thousands of tourists. *Fri–Mon 11am–5pm | admission 6 euros | Via dei Renai 37 | www.museivicifiorentini.comune.fi.it/bardini*

5 MUSEO ZOOLOGICO "LA SPECOLA"
(137 D–E4) (*M E6*)

The former observatory, *La Specola,* now houses a zoological collection, which will also fascinate kids. It includes stuffed animals, from tarantulas to giant tortoises, plus an interesting display of butterflies. Don't miss the – albeit quirky – INSIDER TIP anatomy department. It shows over 1,400 at times breathtakingly life-like wax models of human organs and replicas of entire "skinned" bodies laid out in glass cabinets, some on satin. The majority of the anatomical specimens were fashioned by Clemente Susini between 1775 and 1814 in the museum's own wax modelling workshop, and were used originally to teach medical students. *June–Sept Tue–Sun 10.30am–5.30pm,*

Oct–May Tue–Sun 9.30am–4.30pm | admission 6 euros | Via Romana 17 | www.msn.unifi.it

6 PALAZZO PITTI ●
(137 E4) (*M E–F6*)

The core building of this great palace was built for Florentine merchant Luca

CITY SIGHTSEEING

City-Sightseeing Firenze (www.city-sightseeing.it/it/firenze) offers two different routes which take you right through town and up into the green hills. They operate on the "hop on – hop off" principle, so you can use the same ticket (from 23 euros) to join and leave the tours as you wish within 1, 2 or 3 days. The buses run every 30 or 60 minutes. Audio guides provide explanations in eight languages. Tickets and route plans are available on the bus or at your hotel.

Relax in its spacious gardens and take in the palace's finest art: Palazzo Pitti

Pitti in 1457. Enlarged gradually over the centuries to its current dimensions – the façade is 205 m (224yd) long – the palace was home to the grand dukes of Tuscany until 1859. When Florence was Italy's capital (1865–71), King Victor Emanuel II resided here. Today, the Palazzo Pitti and its adjacent buildings accommodate seven museums and collections. The private painting collection of the grand dukes in the left wing of the palace formed the basis for the *Galleria Palatina* (Palatine Gallery); after the Uffizi, the most important repository of paintings in Florence. The walls of 30 magnificently appointed rooms are literally covered with famous examples of European painting. Highlights of the collection include works by Titian, Raphael, Tintoretto, Giorgione, Rubens, Caravaggio, van Dyck and Velázquez.

On the right-hand side of the upper floor are the *Appartamenti Reali* (Royal Apartments): truly fit for a king. The *Galleria d'Arte Moderna* (Modern Art Gallery) is located on the top floor. In 30 rooms, only some of which are open to the public, the entire spectrum of Tuscan painting of the 18th to 20th centuries is on display. Be sure to take a look at the works of the *Macchiaioli Movement* (painters of *macchie* – spots and patches), contemporaries of the Impressionists.

The *Museo degli Argenti* (Silver Museum), also called *Tesoro dei Granduchi,* is housed in rooms which were decorated for the wedding of Ferdinand II and Vittoria della Rovere in 1634. It contains the Medici silver as well as objects in gold, precious stones and ivory. In the palace wing accessible through the *Giardino di Boboli* (see p. 54) is the *Palazzina della*

Meridiana, now the home of the *Museo della Moda e del Costume*. It boasts costumes and clothing from the Renaissance until the present day.

In the Cavalier's Garden, the Medici grand dukes used to breed silkworms; today it houses the *Museo delle Porcellane* (Porcelain Museum) with a must-see collection of famous-name pieces from the 18th and 19th centuries. *Tue–Sun 8.15am–6.50pm | admission 8.50 euros | tel. 05 52 38 86 11 | Piazza Pitti 1 | www.uffizi.it/palazzo-pitti*

▨ SANTA FELICITA (130 B6) (*⌖ F6*)

What was probably the first Christian church in Florence stood on this site on the Piazza Santa Felicita, directly behind the Ponte Vecchio. The interior of its successor, rebuilt in 1739 in the high Baroque style, contains two Mannerist

gems: the altarpiece showing the *Deposition from the Cross* and the fresco of the *Annunciation* by Pontormo (1525–28). If you're lucky, you may encounter Cristina Lombardi on Fridays. She enjoys showing visitors the nave and the prayer room of the Grand Dukes of the Medici family which connects to the *Corridoio Vasariano*. *Mon–Sat 9.30am–12.30pm and 3.30pm–5pm | Piazza Santa Felicita 3 | www.santafelicitafirenze.it*

▨ SANTA MARIA DEL CARMINE/ CAPPELLA BRANCACCI (137 D3) (*⌖ E5–6*)

The fine church with its plain, rough-cut stone façade (under restoration) can boast a great treasure of Renaissance painting: the frescoes in the *Cappella Brancacci* depicting scenes from the life

Harmonic proportions: Santo Spirito is one of the most magnificent Renaissance churches in Florence

of St Peter. When the original church of the Carmelite Order (from 1268) was almost completely destroyed by fire in 1771, this chapel at the end of the right transept remained untouched by the flames. You can access it today through the courtyard, to the right of the facade. The 15-part *fresco cycle*, begun in 1423 by Masolino da Panicale and Masaccio, was completed in 1483 by Filippino Lippi. Masaccio's frescoes in particular (mostly on the left-hand wall of the chapel) are considered to have paved the way for subsequent artistic developments, due to their inspired depiction of light and shadow and the geometric arrangement of the human figures. Following painstaking restoration work, the frescoes have been returned to their original colourful brilliance. *Chapel: Mon and Wed–Sat 10am–5pm, Sun 1pm–5pm by appointment only | tel. 05 52 76 82 24 | admission 6 euros | Piazza del Carmine 14 | www.museivicifiorentini.comune.fi.it/brancacci*

9 SANTO SPIRITO
(130 A5–6) (*𝄞 E6*)

The Augustinians of Santo Spirito settled here in the mid-13th century, and the school they ran soon became a centre for Humanist studies. The church was built between 1438 and 1482 according to plans by Brunelleschi, and is characterised by its well proportioned, yet unadorned façade. The interior, with its 47 grey sandstone columns, impresses with its clear lines, broken only by the Baroque baldachin altar. Don't miss the wooden INSIDER TIP crucifix by Michelangelo – commands the scene from the centre of the church since 2017 and can be viewed from all angles – and an altarpiece by Filippino Lippi (1488) in the fifth chapel of the right transept. In the former refectory, which is accessed on the left of the facade, Andrea Orcagna

painted frescoes depicting the Last Supper (1360) and the Crucifixion. In front of the church, the many bars and eateries on the *Piazza Santo Spirito* make it a popular meeting place in Oltrarno. *Mon/Tue, Thu–Fri 9.30am–12.30pm and 4pm–5.30pm, Sat/Sun 11.30 am–12.30pm and 4pm–5.30pm | Piazza Santo Spirito 29 | www.basilicasantospirito.it*

10 TORRE SAN NICCOLÒ
(138 A4) (*𝄞 G6*)

The perfect spot for a selfie: scale the steep stairs of one of the last preserved of the city's medieval gate towers to a height of 45 m/148 ft. Visits are limited to 15 people at a time so you have a great opportunity to get the best photos. *Mid June–Aug 5pm–8pm, Sept 4pm–7pm | admission 4 euros | Piazza Giuseppe Poggi | www.musefirenze.it*

MORE SIGHTS

CERTOSA SAN LORENZO DI GALLUZZO
(141 D3) (*𝄞 0*)

Built in 1314, the Carthusian monastery is an architectural gem with cloisters, a library, monk's cells, underground passages and chapels. It's worth a visit just to see Pontormo's Mannerist frescoes and the panel paintings in the Pinacoteca by Andrea del Sarto. In return for a donation, Cistercian monks will show visitors around the complex. *Tue–Sat 0am, 11am, 3pm, 4pm, 5pm, Sun 3pm, 4pm, 5pm, winter: Tue–Sat 10am and 11am, Sun 3pm and 4pm | bus 37*

FORTEZZA DA BASSO
(133 D–E4) (*𝄞 E–F3*)

Upon the Medici's return from exile, Duke Alessandro de' Medici commissioned ar-

An unstressed end of the day on the Piazzale Michelangelo

chitect Antonio Sangallo in 1532 with the construction of this massive, star-shaped fortress at the southern end of the city to be better prepared for possible people's revolts. Twice a year it hosts the large international fair for men's fashions, *Pitti Uomo (www.pittimmagine.com)*, as well as other trade exhibitions, congresses and events. *Viale Filippo Strozzi 1 | bus 1, 2, 4, 6, 8, 11, 12, 13, 14, 17, 20, 23, 28*

MEDICI VILLAS (141 D–E2) (𝒲)

Florence in the 15th century was an over-populated place with narrow passages and dark and gloomy palaces which is why the rich sought refuge in the surrounding hillside. From the beginning of the 16th century, affluent villas were built with grand, symmetrical gardens offering panoramic views of the landscape beyond. The gently rolling hillside is now replaced by residential areas and factories, yet the buildings have stood the test of time, and most of the gardens too. Two of these Medici villas are nestled in the hills bordering the city and are worth a visit, especially for avid gardeners. The best way of getting there is on the bus routes 2 and 28 from the Santa Maria Novella railway station which takes approx. 30 minutes.

Did you know that Botticelli's famous "Primavera" and the "Birth of Venus" paintings – today the main attraction at the Uffizi – once hung in the *Villa Medicea di Castello (Nov–Feb 8.30am–4.30pm, March and Oct 8.30am–5.30pm, April–Sept. 8.30am–6.30pm, closed 2nd and 3rd Mon in the month | free admission | Via di Castello 47 | Sestese Leo France bus stop | www.polomusealetoscana.beni culturali.it)*? The villa fell into the hands of the Medici family in 1480 who transformed it into a royal residence. Today, it houses the headquarters of the Accademia della Crusca and is only open for study purposes. However its garden is open to the public and is a textbook example of the *giardino all'italiana,* only second in beauty to the Boboli Gardens.

Visitors are welcome to view the interiors of the *Villa Medicea La Petraia (Nov–Feb 8.30am–4.30pm, March and Oct 8.30am–5.30pm, April–Sept 8.30am–6.30pm, closed 2nd and 3rd Mon in the month | free admission | Via della Petraia 40 | Sestese 03 bus stop | www.polomuse*

aletoscana.beniculturali.it). The residence was once the love nest of Italy's first King Vittorio Emanuele II and his mistress, the Bella Rosina, and was therefore transformed into a residence fit for royalty. In 1544, Cosimo I de' Medici inherited the building and lavished it further over the decades to include a covered courtyard decorated with splendid frescoes. Three large ✂ terraces provide panoramic views over the valley and Florence.

PARCO DELLE CASCINE
(132 A–B5) (*ₐ B–C 3–4*)

Covering an area of 1.6 km², the park is located on a promontory between the rivers Arno and Mugnone. It is the site of the *Ippodromo del Visarno,* Florence's horse racing track, with bridle paths and various sports facilities. *Piazzale delle Cascine | bus 17, 28, 29, 30, 35, 60, C2, C3 | tram 1*

INSIDERTIP ▶ PIAZZALE MICHELANGELO
● ✂ (138 B4) (*ₐ H6*)

This huge observation plateau is perched high up above the Arno in the south of the city, with café, restaurant, bar and plenty of parking spaces. The fabulous view from here is much loved by residents and tourists alike. A highly conspicuous bronze copy of Michelangelo's *David* and the *Four Allegories* at his feet dominate the square. *Bus 12, 13*

SAN MINIATO AL MONTE ★ ✂
(138 B5) (*ₐ H7*)

Visible for miles around, this treasure of Romanesque architecture stands on a hill south of the Arno. The view over Florence from the square in front of the church is truly fabulous. A church has stood on this spot since the days of Charlemagne; presumably built to mark the grave of St Minias, who died a martyr in 250 AD. His remains are kept in a shrine in the crypt. The façade of today's basilica (1018–1207)

is clad in white Carrara marble and green serpentine. Floor, choir screen and pulpit are ornamented with exquisite marble inlays. The apse mosaic from 1297 showing the *Enthroned Christ* has been restored on many occasions. At the end of the nave is the free-standing *Cappella del Crocefisso* by Michelozzo (1448), its barrel-vaulted ceiling decorated with rosettes and blue majolica tiles by Luca della Robbia. The altarpieces (around 1396) came from the atelier of Agnolo Gaddi. The left-hand nave contains the *Cappella del Cardinale del Portogallo,* whose tomb was designed by Rossellino; the chapel ceiling with circular reliefs made of coloured, glazed terracotta – are by Luca della Robbia (1461–66). Between 1373 and 1552 – and again today – the church and the adjacent *Palazzo dei Vescovi* belonged to the Olivetan Order, a Benedictine Congregation, whose ● vespers chants can be heard in the church every day at around 5.30pm. *Daily 8.15am–8pm, winter Mon–Sat 9.30am–1pm and 3pm–7pm, Sun 8.15am–7pm | Via Monte alle Croci | www.sanminiatoal monte.it | bus 12, 13*

SINAGOGA/MUSEO EBRAICO
(138 B2) (*ₐ H4–5*)

Building work on the Synagogue in Florence was completed in 1882, a fine example of neo-Moorish architecture. The interior is decorated entirely with frescoes. The mosaics, stained-glass windows and ornamentations in bronze and wood are also worthy of note. The story of the Jews in Florence is documented on the first floor through photographs, paintings and ritual objects. *June–Sept Sun–Thu 10am–6.30pm, Fri 10am–5pm, Oct–May Sun–Thu 10am–5.30pm, Fri 10am–3pm, closed Sat and on Jewish holidays | admission 6.50 euros | Via Farini 4/6 | www.jewishtuscany.it | bus 6, 14, 19, 23, 31, 32, C1, C2*

FOOD & DRINK

Have you ever tried *crostini*, toasted white bread spread with a delicious liver paste or *fagioli all'uccelletto*, white beans with sage in a tomato sauce or maybe even a *bistecca alla fiorentina*, a 4 cm/1.6 inches thick, 800 g T-bone beef steak, barbecued and rubbed with salt and pepper and *basta?* A visit to Tuscany would not be complete without eating these finest local specialities! When Italians have something to celebrate, they go out to eat. So if you want to compete, bear in mind the following points: Most eateries (whether a ristorante, trattoria or osteria) are open from 12.30pm–2.30pm and 7.30pm–10.30pm. Pizza is usually only available – except as *pizza a taglio* to takeaway – only in the evenings., even at pizzerias. There is a wide variety of establishments in the city centre which offer a *menù fisso,* usually a three-course meal for a cheap set price. However, the food they serve often has little in common with the celebrated Tuscan cuisine made from fresh, seasonal ingredients. The better option is to order a *panino* filled with ingredients of your choice at a good bar or ordinary food store.

Meat dishes are generally grilled or fried, vegetable side dishes *(contorni),* which you often have to order separately, are gently steamed and then refined with a dash of olive oil. As for drinks, wine and/or water *gassata* (carbonated) or *naturale* (non-carbonated) are served with your meal. And feel free to ask for the *vino della casa* (house wine) which is also available in 1/4 or 1/2 litre carafes. Although res-

More than pizza and pasta – in Florentine restaurants, what counts are fresh ingredients and the Tuscan culinary tradition

taurants rarely have a separate children's menu, you can always ask for half a portion of pasta *(mezza porzione)*. Guests are asked to wait at the entrance to the restaurant before being seated. Another thing you should be aware of is that a charge per person for *coperto* (bread and cover charge) is almost always added to the price of the meal; this varies between 1.50 and 3.50 euros. On top of this there is a *servizio* (service charge) of 10–15 percent. Tipping is also customary of around 10 percent. And whatever you drink in a bar, remember that prices are often doubled if you sit down rather than remain standing at the bar. *Bon appetito!*

CAFÉS

CAFFÈ PITTI (130 A6) *(𝄞 E6)*
Opposite the Palazzo Pitti, with Art-Deco furnishings, sofas and good wine. Between noon and 5pm there's a three-course menu for 15 euros, in the evenings delicacies à la carte. *Daily noon–11pm | Piazza Pitti 9 | www.caffepitti.it*

Even with increasing competition, the ice cream from Vivoli is still legendary

CHIAROSCURO (131 D4) (🛱 F5)
A run-of-the-mill Italian bar at the heart of the city centre, but with lots of coffee varieties, good cocktails and a delicious lunchtime menu. *Daily 7.30am–9.30pm | Via del Corso 36r | www.chiaroscuro.it*

DITTA ARTIGIANALE (131 D5) (🛱 G5)
This casual hipster café is a great place to try and also buy all different varieties of coffee – they have roasted coffee beans from around the world. Run by the Italian barista champion Francesco Sanapo, the roaster also offers courses specialising in coffee beans. *Daily 8am–midnight | Via dei Neri 21r | www.dittaartigianale.it*

GILLI (130 C4) (🛱 F5)
Founded in 1733 and still popular, especially thanks to its excellent cappuccino. Elegant ambience, historical charm. *Wed–Mon 7.30am–1am | Via Roma 1 | www.gilli.it*

GIUBBE ROSSE (130 C4) (🛱 F5)
Bar and nostalgic café. Around 1900, this was the haunt of the literary and artistic crowd. Today, small concerts, literary events and exhibitions are organised. The waiters in their red waistcoats *(giubbe rosse)* also serve menus. *Daily 10am–1am | Piazza della Repubblica 13r | www.giubberosse.it*

RIVOIRE ● (130 C4) (🛱 F5)
Expensive (if you sit down at a table), but in a class of its own. The Florentine institution serves a delicious INSIDER TIP *cioccolata calda con panna* (hot chocolate with whipped cream). *Tue–Sun 8am–midnight | Piazza della Signoria 5 | www.rivoire.it*

ENOTECHE & SNACK BARS

ARÀ (134 A6) (🛱 G4)
Excellent Sicilian snack for between meals! *Daily 10am–10pm | Via degli Alfani 127r*

LA DIVINA ENOTECA (130 C1) (*ম F4*)
In the heart of the city, the friendly proprietors Bianca and Livio offer excellent wines – and a bite to eat. *Tue–Sun 10.30am–9pm | Via Panicale 19r | tel. 0 55 29 27 23 | www.ladivinaenoteca.it*

DORSODURO (133 F3) (*ম G3*)
Andrea comes from Venice and has brought the Venetian culinary tradition of *cicchetti* (snacks or side dishes) to Florence. These are served with an excellent *Spritz Veneziano.* A crowd favourite is the traditional *baccalà mantecato (*stockfish). The bar is tiny but offers outdoor seating. *Mon–Sat 5pm–10pm | Via San Gallo 41r | tel. 05 55 27 40 54*

'INO (130 C5) (*ম F5*)
Here, in a tiny side street behind the Piazza della Signoria, you can create a kind of do-it-yourself gourmet sandwich and enjoy a good glass of wine to wash it down. *Daily noon–4.30pm | Via dei Georgofili 3r–7r | www.inofirenze.com*

LA MÉNAGÈRE ★ (130 C2) (*ম F4*)
Be it an early-morning cappuccino and newspaper for breakfast, a delicious *panino* or warm snack for lunch, a late-afternoon piece of cake, an *aperitivo della casa* or a tasty dinner, this concept restaurant-store is a casual, hip, cosy, romantic and elegant place also selling tableware and fresh flowers. There is even live music at the weekends. *Daily 7am–2am | Via de' Ginori 8r | tel. 05 50 75 06 00 | www.lamenagere.it*

INSIDERTIP► PROCACCI (130 B3) (*ম F5*)
If your palate calls for a glass of good white wine and an exquisite truffle pâté sandwich, rather than sweet snacks, and if you favour a slightly genteel atmosphere, you'll go crazy for this place! *Mon–Sat 10am–8pm | Via Tornabuoni 64r | www.procacci1885.it*

VIVANDA ☻ (137 D3) (*ম E5*)
A very healthy place! Everything is organic – 120 different wines and very

---

★ **Vivoli**
Try what, according to the Florentines, is the best ice cream in town!
→ p. 66

★ **La Ménagère**
Bistro-restaurant, café, designer store, florist and cocktail bar all in one → p. 65

★ **Enoteca Pinchiorri**
For special occasions: culinary delights are accompanied by the most prestigious wines → p. 67

★ **Cibrèo Ristorante**
Culinary empire in the market quarter of Sant'Ambrogio → p. 67

★ **La Giostra**
Simply delicious: fantastic dishes and a good assortment of wines → p. 67

★ **Obicà Mozzarella Bar**
The variety of tasty Mozzarella creations will surprise you → p. 69

★ **Omero**
The country and its people: you can enjoy both in this historic restaurant → p. 67

★ **Il Santo Bevitore**
A mixture of tradition and modernity: a fun place to dine → p. 70

★ **Fiaschetteria Trattoria Mario**
Typical Florentine dishes in a tiny restaurant tucked behind the market → p. 70

MARCO POLO HIGHLIGHTS

tempting dishes. *Daily 10am–3pm and 6pm–midnight | Via Santa Monaca 7 | www.vivandafirenze.it*

ICE CREAM PARLOURS

INSIDER**TIP** GROM (130 C3) (*∅ F5*)
The know-how behind making the ice cream comes from Turin; the ingredients from all over the globe. Centrally located between Duomo and Palazzo Vecchio. *April–Oct 10.30am–midnight, Nov–March until 11pm | Via del Campanile/Via delle Oche | www.grom.it*

PARCO CARABÈ (131 D1) (*∅ G4*)
Antonio arguably serves the city's best Sicilian *granita:* crushed ice mixed with fresh fruits. *Daily 9am–1.30am, winter 10am–7.30pm | Via Ricasoli 60 | www.parcocarabe.it*

VIVOLI ★ ● (131 E4) (*∅ G5*)
Diese *gelateria* is reputed to be Florence's best ice-cream parlour. You will be spoilt for choice with over 40 flavours to choose from. *Tue–Sun until midnight, Nov–Mar until 9pm | Via Isola delle Stinche 7 | www.vivoli.it*

FAVOURITE EATERIES

A seaside experience
When you eat fish in the *Fishing Lab Alle Murate* **(131 D4)** (*∅ G5*) *(daily | Via del Proconsolo 16r | tel. 0 55 24 06 18 | www.fishinglab.it/firenze | Moderate–Expensive)* – whether cooked, raw, cured, with head and fins or sashimi – you will feel like at the seaside, walking bare foot along the sand with the sea breeze in your hair. The walls of this contemporary-styled restaurant are lined with original frescoes, including the INSIDER**TIP** only authentic portrait of Dante.

Bistecca with operatic outbursts
Where? At the *Osteria dei Pazzi* **(131 E4)** (*∅ G5*) *(Tue–Sun | Via dei Lavatoi 3 | tel. 05 52 34 48 80 | Moderate)*! The owner, Paolo, is prone to bursting out in song and the restaurant serves a delicious 5-cm thick *bistecca alla fiorentina*. If you come with a large appetite, let him arrange a plate of antipasti for you or order a generous portion of pasta – both are delicious.

Polished establishment
Housed in a former silver polish factory, the *Piazza del Vino* **(139 E2)** (*∅ K5*) *(daily | Via della Torretta 18r | tel. 0 55 67 14 04 | www.piazzadelvino.weebly.com | Moderate–Expensive)* serves dishes originating from all over Italy. Offering a cool and no-frills atmosphere and food, this place is steeped in Florence tradition and over 25,000 bottles of wine line its walls. Located slightly outside the main city centre, but the journey is well worth it.

Market centre
Nerbone **(130 B–C1)** (*∅ F4*) *(Mon–Sat 7am–2pm | Via dell'Ariento | Budget)* is everything but cool. Forge your way past the lunchtime crowds to taste this stall's traditional and feisty dishes. It can get extremely crowded and loud but the stall in the Mercato Centrale remains a firm favourite among Florentines who come for *lampredotto* (tripe), *inzimino* (fish stew) or simply a roast beef.

RESTAURANTS: EXPENSIVE

CIBRÈO RISTORANTE ⭐
(138 B2) *(📖 H5)*

Fabio Picchi has found a way of introducing everyone to the finest Tuscan cuisine – without a trace of pasta on the menu. He also relishes the opportunity to present the changing dishes of the day in person. The somewhat cheaper *Cibreino* next door is also run by Picchi (see below). Reservation required. *Tue–Sun | Via Andrea del Verrochio 8r | tel. 05 52 34 11 00 | www.cibreo.com*

ENOTECA PINCHIORRI ⭐
(138 A2) *(📖 G5)*

If you have reason to celebrate, head to this gourmet temple for a meal cooked by one of the five female chefs in the world to be awarded three Michelin stars. It is rated as one of Europe's best restaurants. The fact that 150,000 wine bottles are stored in the cellar speaks for itself. Sit back and enjoy the experience – but be prepared for the pricy bill at the end. *Tue–Sat evenings only | Via Ghibellina 87 | tel. 0 55 24 27 77 | www.enotecapinchiorri.com*

LA GIOSTRA ⭐ (131 E3) *(📖 G5)*

Excellent cuisine and splendid choice of wines. Restaurateur and chef, the Grand Duke of Soldano serves his guests in person every evening! *Mon–Fri and Sat evenings | Borgo Pinti 10r | tel. 0 55 24 13 41 | www.ristorantelagiostra.com*

OMERO ⭐ ● 🌿 (141 E3) *(📖 F8)*

Fine regional specialities. You enter the dining room (with its fantastic view) through the *bottega,* where hams and salami hang from the ceiling and you can also get yourself a simple ham sandwich. Galileo Galilei once lived opposite. *Daily | Via Pian dei Giullari 11r | tel. 0 55 22 00 53 | www.ristoranteomero.it*

La Menagère: laid-back concept restaurant

RESTAURANTS: MODERATE

4 LEONI (130 B6) *(📖 F6)*

Trademark trattoria where you can enjoy very good home-made pasta and *bistecca alla fiorentina! Closed Wed lunchtime | Via de' Vellutini 1/Via Toscanella | tel. 0 55 21 85 62 | www.4leoni.com*

CIBREINO (138 B2) *(📖 H5)*

A spin-off of the fine-dining *Cibrèo* (see above). The meals here are simpler and served on wooden tables. No reservations possible. *Sept–July Tue–Sun 12.50pm–2.30pm and 7pm–11.30pm | Via dei Macci 122r | www.edizioniteatrodel salecibreofirenze.it*

LOCAL SPECIALITIES

arista alla fiorentina – grilled fillet of pork with rosemary and garlic

baccalà alla fiorentina – stockfish in tomato sauce with basil

biscotti di Prato (cantucci) – almond biscuits to be dipped in *vin santo,* a sweet dessert wine (photo right)

bistecca alla fiorentina – a 3.5-cm (1 1/2 in) thick T-bone steak (photo left)

carciofi fritti – fried quartered artichokes

cinghiale (coniglio) in umido – wild boar or rabbit in tomato sauce

crostini toscani – toasted bread spread with a paste made of chicken liver, capers and fresh herbs

fettunta – toasted slices of white bread: in summer with tomatoes and basil; in winter with garlic and drizzled with freshly pressed olive oil

lesso (bollito misto) con salsa verde – boiled meat (beef, tongue, chicken) with green herb sauce

panzanella – a summer salad served on soaked white bread and tomatoes

pappa al pomodoro – luke-warm tomato and bread soup

pollo al mattone – chicken, pressed flat under a brick and roasted over a wood fire

ribollita – re-heated vegetable soup with white beans and bread

tagliata – steak, stripped from the bone and cut into strips

tagliatelle alla lepre (al cinghiale) – ribbon noodles with hare or wild boar ragout

trippa alla fiorentina – calf tripe with tomato sauce

INSIDER TIP COCO LEZZONE
(130 B4) *(∅ E5)*
One of the places to be. Florentine society people squeeze into the cramped interior to enjoy superlative cuisine. *Closed Sun and Tue evenings | Via del Parioncino 26r | tel. 0 55 28 71 78*

ENZO E PIERO (130 B1) *(∅ F4)*
Ask Aldo for the special of the day. This establishment has been serving great food for nearly 90 years. The *tortellacci* are a delicious *primo,* followed by one of the game dishes. *Mon–Sat | Via Faenza 105r | tel. 0 55 21 49 01 | www.trattor iaenzoepiero.it*

IL GUSCIO (136 C3) *(∅ D5)*
A typical trattoria: good cooking (traditional Tuscan cuisine in this case) and a long wine list. *Tue–Sat evenings only | Via dell'Orto 49a | tel. 0 55 22 44 21 | www.il-guscio.it*

LUNGARNO 23 (131 D6) (*M G6*)

For meat lovers: Everything from the Chianina breed of cow: carpaccio, roast beef, steak tartare and exquisite hamburgers. *Mon–Sat | Lungarno Torrigiani 23 | tel. 05 52 34 59 57 | www.lungarno23.it*

INSIDER TIP DA MIMMO
(133 F5) (*M G3*)

Mimmo is committed to using only fresh ingredients for his excellent dishes – one more reason to come for a meal to this beautiful 17th-century theatre! *Closed Sat lunchtime, Sun | Via San Gallo 57–59r | tel. 0 55 48 10 30 | www.ristorantedamimmo.it*

OBICÀ MOZZARELLA BAR ★
(130 B3) (*M F5*)

The elegant Palazzo Tornabuoni is the place to eat the best Mozzarella in town. If you would like to find out more about Southern Italian cheese making, you can also take part in a cheese-tasting session. *Daily 8am–11pm | Via dei Tornabuoni 16 | tel. 05 52 77 35 01 | www.obica.com*

OLIVIA (130 B6) (*M E–F6*)

Oil, to be precise pure Tuscan olive oil, is the main ingredient of every meal served here. Food is also available to take away. Skin-care products made of olive oil are also available. *Piazza Pitti 14r | tel. 05 52 67 03 59 | www.oliviafirenze.com*

OSTARIA DEI CENTOPOVERI
(130 A3) (*M E4*)

Taste for yourself the culinary art of chef Nicola Ferrara – and be sure to try one of the desserts – you will remember it for a long time! *Wed–Mon | Via Palazzuolo 31 | tel. 0 55 21 88 46 | www.centopoveri.*

L'OV 🌱 (137 D3) (*M E5*)

In a delightful greenhouse setting, this restaurant is paradise for strict vegetarians as well as gluten-free eaters. Simone Bernacchiani serves up the city's best veggie burger. *Mon–Sat | Piazza del Carmine 4r | tel. 05 52 05 23 88 | www.oster iavegetariana.it*

Il Guscio offers traditional *cucina fiorentina* in an authentic atmosphere

Traditional surroundings and good regional fare: Sostanza detto "Il Troia"

IL SANTO BEVITORE ⭐ (137 D3) (🗺 E5)

Delicious starters, including various types of ham and marinated or grilled vegetables. And to follow, choose the *tartara of* Chianina beef or one of the good fish dishes. Excellent value for money. *Daily except Sun lunchtime | Via Santo Spirito 66r | tel. 0 55 21 12 64 | www.ilsantobevitore.com*

SOSTANZA DETTO "IL TROIA" (130 A3) (🗺 E5)

Chagall was among those who came to this trattoria, founded in 1869, to savour its Tuscan specialities. *Mon–Fri, April/May, Sept/Oct also Sat | Via del Porcellana 25r | tel. 0 55 21 26 91*

TRATTORIA DELL'ORTO (136 C3) (🗺 D5)

Bright interior, pleasant service, Tuscan fare. In summer you can eat outside. *Wed–Mon | Via dell'Orto 35a | tel. 0 55 22 41 48 | www.trattoriadellorto.com*

DOLCE VEGAN 🌐 (134 A4) (🗺 G3)

The finest vegan dishes are prepared in this tiny organic bistro. The desserts are particularly appetising! *Daily noon–3pm and 7pm–midnight | Via San Gallo 92r | mobile tel. 32 88 2112 20 | www.dolcevegan.it*

FIASCHETTERIA NUVOLI (130 C3) (🗺 F4)

Don't be put off by the size of this tiny cellar diner. This is a great place to have a snack – best at lunchtime – in the company of Florentines. *Mon–Sat 8am–9pm | Piazza dell'Olio 15 | tel. 05 52 39 66 16*

FIASCHETTERIA TRATTORIA MARIO ⭐ (130 A4) (🗺 F4)

Tiny, typical trattoria near the Mercato San Lorenzo, always full to bursting. Small selection of local dishes. *Mon–Sat lunchtime only | Via Rosina 2r | tel. 0 55 218550 | www.trattoriamario.com*

INSIDER TIP GOZZI SERGIO
(130 C2) (*M F4*)

Keep things simple - this friendly tratto- ria on the Piazza San Lorenzo has been serving the same traditional meals for decades. Dining is at cosy tables where guests sit with strangers around the same table to enjoy the delicious food. *Mon–Sat lunchtime only | Piazza San Lor- enzo 8 | tel. 0 55 28 19 41*

INSIDER TIP MERCATO CENTRALE
(130 B–C1) (*M F4*)

The stall owners of the first-floor food mile in the old market hall are proud of the fact that they only sell seasonal and regional produce and use them in their dishes. Ultimate culinary enjoyment for all tastes - and the perfect place to meet up and dine with friends. *Daily 10am– midnight | Piazza del Mercato Centrale | Via dell'Ariento 10–14 | www.mercatoce ntrale.it*

OSTERIA SAN NICCOLÒ
(138 A4) (*M G6*)

Friendly osteria far from the tourist crowds: Excellent Florentine cuisine is served at affordable prices until 12 mid- night. *Daily | Via San Niccolò 60r | tel. 05 52 34 28 36 | osteriasanniccolo.it*

ROSE'S (130 B4) (*M F5*)

Trendy. A small place valued by business- men, with a good light lunch near the Via Tornabuoni. *Mon–Sat noon–1.30am | Via del Parione 26r | tel. 0 55 28 70 90 | www.roses.it*

TRATTORIA LA CASALINGA
(137 E3) (*M E6*)

Always full, always good, always the place to be. Very modest trattoria, dishing up traditional Tuscan fare. Book in advance! *Mon–Sat | Via dei Michelozzi 9r | tel. 0 55 21 86 24 | www.trattorialacasalinga.it*

TRATTORIA SANT'AGOSTINO
(137 D3) (*M E6*)

Popular Oltrarno trattoria. You can get a full lunchtime menu, including dessert, for only 13 euros. *Tue–Sun | Via Sant' Agostino 23r | tel. 0 55 210 2 08 | www. santagostinofirenze.com*

IL VEGETARIANO ◎ (133 F5) (*M G3*)

Vegetarian (organic) trattoria: small, good quality and value for money. *Tue–Sun, Sat/ Sun lunch only | Via delle Ruote 30r | tel. 0 55 475 0 30 | www.il-vegetariano.it*

LOW BUDGET

A tasty roll (*panino*) will take care of those hunger pangs between meals, e.g. at the *Pizzicheria Guadagni* **(131 E4)** (*M G5*) (*Mon–Sat 8am–8pm | Via Isola delle Stinche 4*) or in the *Oste- ria de l'Ortolano* **(131 D1)** (*M G4*) (*Mon– Fri 10am–8pm, Sat until 2pm | Via deg- li Alfani 91r*). *I Fratellini* **(130 C4)** (*M F5*) (*Mon–Sat | Via dei Cimatori 38r*) be- tween Duomo and Piazza della Signoria is also famous for its *panini*.

Quick, cheap, delicious: Join the queue at the deli counter at *Anti- co Vinaio* **(131 D5)** (*M G5*) (*Via dei Neri 65r | www.allanticovinaio.com*) for a *panino* or – even better – a *schi- acciata* with the filling of your choice.

Cooked offal is a speciality of Florence: Give the *trippa* a try from one of the value-for-money ● stands on the *Pi- azza dei Cimatori* **(131 D4)** (*M E5*) or next to the *Loggia del Mercato Nuovo* **(130 C4)** (*M F5*) in the *Via Calimaruzza*!

SHOPPING

CITY WHERE TO START?
Piazza della Repubblica
(130 C3–4) (*M F5*): Shopping hub
in the city: If you want to see the
latest from the world of haute couture, stroll over to the luxury shopping triangle Via della Vigna Vec-
chia/Via Tornabuoni/Via Strozzi:
Armani, Bulgari, Cavalli... on to
Zegna: The ABC of fashion spelled
out! If that's beyond your means,
take a walk along the narrow
streets in the opposite direction,
where there's something for every
budget. Electric minibus C1 and C2,
bus 6 and 11; car parking: Stazione
Santa Maria Novella.

A dose of retail therapy in Florence is an aesthetic pleasure – but it could also be an expensive one.

Fashion is definitely the absolute top tip when it comes to shopping, especially during the sales *(saldi)* in January/Feb-ruary and in July/August. Pay attention, though; Italian clothing sizes can be con-fusing to say the least. As a very rough guide, Italian size 42 is equivalent to UK size 10/US size 8. Are you into gold, silver, precious stones or cutlery? If so, head for the area around the Ponte Vecchio, where you'll find not only the real thing, but also imaginative fashion jewellery. Crossing the Arno, you enter the district of Oltrarno, which kicks off with the *Borgo San Jacopo* and its extravagant boutiques, while the territory of the antique dealers

From exquisite boutiques to rustic markets – Florence has something unique for every budget and taste!

extends between Via Maggio, Via Santo Spirito and Borgo San Frediano.

Normal opening hours are *Mon–Sat 9am–1pm and 3.30pm–7.30pm.* The shops in the city centre do not usually close for lunch; some are even open on Sundays. Food shops are closed on Wednesday afternoons; all other types of shop on Monday mornings. In July/August, many shops close on Saturday afternoons – except fashion boutiques and department stores. Some shops close altogether for two weeks in mid-August.

ANTIQUES

ATELIER MELISSA GENTILE
(130 A3) (*ω E5*)

A number of shops are grouped around the pretty inner courtyard of the Palazzo Fossombroni. *Closed Sat | Via dei Fossi 7b/r*

CASA WOLF (137 D1) (*ω E5*)

Over many years, Renato, a surgeon, collected items of furniture. Today, these antiques are up for sale. *Borgo San Frediano 151r | www.casawolf.it*

All the delicacies of Tuscany packed into one stall at Perini

ART, GALLERIES & MORE

FABRIANO BOUTIQUE (131 D4) (*ⓜ F5*)
There are no tacky souvenirs on sale in this modern stationery boutique, only luxurious and high-quality writing paper and pens. Fabriano has been making paper since 1264. Iain Anthony offers his professional service and will explain the history behind this age-old tradition. *Via del Corso 59r | www.fabrianoboutique.it*

NENCIONI ★ (131 D4) (*ⓜ F5*)
Over 2 million copperplate prints from different periods, showing various motifs – whether maps, vedute, plants or animals. There's sure to be a frame to go with each print, if you wish. *Via della Condotta 25r*

IL TAMARINO (130 A3) (*ⓜ E5*)
Limited editions of original etchings. Francesco can make your own special motif to order. *Via del Moro 46r | www.iltamarino.com*

TORNABUONI ARTE
(138 C4) (*ⓜ H6*)
With its outstanding architecture, the new home of this renowned art gallery is comparable to a small museum. This 500 m² two-storey building mainly organises exhibitions of Italian twentieth century painters. A paradise for collectors and enthusiasts of modern, contemporary art. *Lungarno Benvenuto Cellini 3 | www.tornabuoniarte.it*

ZECCHI
(131 D3) (*ⓜ F5*)
Everything for artists and restorers. This is the place to find exactly those materials the best Renaissance artists used to use. *Via dello Studio 19r | www.zecchi.it*

BOOKSHOPS

GOZZINI
(131 D1) (*ⓜ F4*)
The small, well-kept antiquarian bookshop has rarities and bags of atmosphere to offer. *Via Ricasol 49 | www.gozzini.com*

LA FELTRINELLI LIBRERIE
(130 C3) *(ω F5)*
Huge selection of foreign-language literature. *Via dei Cerretani 40r | www.lafeltrinelli.it*

DELICATESSEN

BOTTEGA DELL'OLIO (130 B5) *(ω F5)*
The finest olive oils and everything else that can be produced from olives. *Piazza del Limbo 2r/Borgo SS. Apostoli | www.labottegadelloliofirenze.it*

EATALY (130 C2) *(ω F4)*
2500m^2/27,000 sq. ft. of Italian food culture in a one-stop food shop: the best produce from every region of Italy, cook books and even cookery courses are available in this store. A touch of the Mediterranean for you to take back home. *Via Martelli 22r | www.firenze.eataly.it*

OLIO RESTAURANT (130 A5) *(ω E5)*
The old shelves are full of delicious specialities to take home with you: olive oil, honey, pasta sauces, wine and much more besides. Or do you fancy a quick bite to eat for lunch? You can also satisfy that desire in this fine palazzo in Oltrarno. *Via Santo Spirito 4 | www.oliorestaurant.it*

PEGNA (131 D3) *(ω F5)*
This delicatessen near the cathedral has been in existence since 1860. Today, it is a supermarket bursting with culinary treats. *Via dello Studio 8 | www.pegna.it*

INSIDERTIP **PERINI** (130 B1) *(ω F4)*
An eldorado in the market hall, offering foods of the highest quality. Have yourself a delicious *panino* made with all your favourite ingredients! *Mercato Centrale | Via dell'Ariento | www.perinigastronomia.it*

VENCHI (130 C4) *(ω F5)*
A feast for the eyes and palate: the finest quality chocolate since 1878 in pralines, bars and the best ice cream! *Via Calimaruzza 18 | also Via Calzaiuoli 65* (130 C3) *(ω F5)* | *www.venchi.com*

DEPARTMENT STORES

COIN (130 C4) *(ω F5)*
Upmarket department store based on the shop-in-the-shop system. Good hosiery department and large sizes – a

★ **Le Pietre nell'Arte**
Inlaid work, just like in the 16th century → p. 77

★ **Sbigoli Terrecotte**
A world of ceramics → p. 78

★ **Nencioni**
Over two million prints in stock → p. 74

★ **Il Bisonte**
All things great and small in finest leather → p. 79

★ **Mercato Centrale**
Eldorado for the gourmet palate → p. 80

★ **Mercato San Lorenzo**
Clothes and much more besides → p. 80

★ **Antico Setificio Fiorentino**
Silk, hand-woven according to historical patterns → p. 76

★ **Loretta Caponi**
Classy underwear – for kids, too → p. 81

MARCO POLO HIGHLIGHTS

rarity in Italy. All kinds of decorative things for the flat in the basement. *Daily 10am–8pm | Via dei Calzaiuoli 56r | www.coin.it*

LA RINASCENTE (130 C3–4) (*ﬃ F5*)

A real shoppers' paradise, from the perfume department to the designer clothes. If you go up to the well-stocked household goods department on the 4th floor, then climb the small flight of stairs on the right, you can enjoy a ● ⠤⠤ INSIDER TIP fantastic view from the roof terrace across the city. *Mon–Sat 10am–9pm, Sun 10.30am–8pm | Piazza della Repubblica | www.larinascente.it*

FABRICS

ANTICO SETIFICIO FIORENTINO ★ ●
(136 C2) (*ﬃ D5*)

Alessandro Pucci has rejuvenated an 18th-century silk-weaving mill in the San Frediano district, where he produces and sells fabulous fabrics featuring antique designs. Not what you'd call cheap, but the ultimate in exclusivity! *Via Bartolini 4 | www.anticosetificiofiorentino.com*

CASA DEI TESSUTI (130 C3) (*ﬃ F5*)

The biggest selection of haute-couture textiles in Florence. The models are presented by means of video projector and then specially made up for you. Approximately 2000 different fabrics are permanently in stock. *Via dei Pecori 20–24r | www.casadeitessuti.com*

FASHION

ALTA ROSA ◍ (133 F5) (*ﬃ G3*)

Stylish women's fashions made from fabrics which are produced according to ecologically sound practices. *Via San Gallo 84r | www.altarosa.it*

ANDREA PALOMBINI (131 E4) (*ﬃ G5*)

Made-to-measure ladies' blouses and gentlemen's shirts fashioned from the most exquisite materials. If your choice is not a perfect fit, it will be altered and sent on within the following two weeks. *Via del Corso 12r | www.andreapalombini.com*

EMILIO PUCCI (130 B4) (*ﬃ F5*)

Headquarters of the Pucci fashion dynasty. The Florentine designer's eccentric fabrics are unmistakable. You should at least take a look at them! *Via Tornabuoni 20/22r | www.emiliopucci.it*

ERMENEGILDO ZEGNA
(130 B4) (*ﬃ E–F5*)

Clothing and accessories for the fashion-conscious man. *ViamTornabuoni 3 | www.zegna.com*

FLÒ ◍ (130 A3) (*ﬃ E5*)

Vintage fashions and accessories plus creations by young designers who believe in sustainability. *Lungarno Corsini 30–34 | www.flo-firenze.org*

LUISA VIA ROMA (130 C3) (*ﬃ F5*)

The Florentine fashion temple: exclusive boutique on two floors with the latest designs, not only from Italian labels. *Via Roma 19–21r | www.luisaviaroma.com*

FLORENTINE CURIOS & SOUVENIRS

ALBERTO COZZI (130 B4) (*ﬃ E–F5*)

This fourth-generation bookbinder and restorer has been boasting the finest craftsmanship since 1908. The shop is famous for its traditional marbled Florentine paper in leather-bound albums and notebooks (stamped with your initials on request) as well as special stationery. When Riccardo has the time, he will marble the paper himself – a real spectacle worth watching. *Via del Parione 35r | www.riccardoluci.com*

CARLO SAITTA (138 B2) (*ℳ H5*)
Hand-made paper, printed with artistic designs. You can even watch the artisan papermakers at work. *Via dell'Agnolo 28*

LA CORALLINA (141 E3) (*ℳ K6*)
All kinds of tastefully designed, hand-made furnishings and fittings! *Lungarno Ferrucci 21 | www.lacorallina-firenze.it*

LEGATORIA LA CARTA (137 D4) (*ℳ E6*)
Omero Benvenuti has been working as a book binder since 1967. His bound diaries and photo albums are works of art in their own right. *Via Romana 58r | www.legatoria-lacarta.com*

OFFICINA PROFUMO-FARMACEUTICA DI SANTA MARIA NOVELLA ● ◐
(130 A2) (*ℳ E4*)
Right on entering, you are captivated by the scent of Tuscan herbs. The Dominicans founded a monastery apothecary here in 1221; nowadays, you can purchase perfumes like the INSIDER TIP *acqua di rose*, which has been distilled here for centuries, soaps and potpourris in these hallowed halls – all made from natural herbs and lipids. Attached is a small museum. *Via della Scala 16 | www.smnovella.com*

ORTIGIA (130 B5) (*ℳ F6*)
The scents and fragrances are intoxicating in this tiny boutique. The packaging alone is reason enough to buy the luxury soaps, lotions and bathing oils made of natural Sicilian ingredients for friends and relatives back home. *Borgo San Jacopo 1 | www.ortigiasicilia.com*

LE PIETRE NELL'ARTE ★
(131 D3) (*ℳ G4*)
Only once you have watched the painstaking work and endless patience of the *artigiani* can you really appreciate the value of this relatively unknown art form. *Florentine Commesso* is a type of mosaic art using semi-precious stones. This craftsmanship has been passed on from father to son since the 16th century to create true works of arts such as broches, jewellery boxes or large table-tops. *Via Ricasoli 59r | www.scarpellimosaici.it*

Finest leather, innovative design: Scuola del Cuoio

"Fresh" is the maxim in the Mercato Centrale whether for flowers or in the new food mile

SBIGOLI TERRECOTTE ⭐
(131 E3) (*📖 G5*)

From painted egg cups or prettily glazed water jugs to enormous hand-crafted terracotta vases from Impruneta – it's all available here. *Via Sant' Egidio 4r | www.sbigoliterrecotte.it*

GLASS, PORCELAIN & SILVER

ARMANDO POGGI (130 C3) (*📖 F5*)

Armando Poggi is one of the old established companies which sell everything you need for a beautifully laid table. *Via dei Calzaiuoli 103r/116r | www.apoggi.com*

INSIDER TIP ▶ MOLERIA LOCCHI
(136 C2) (*📖 D5*)

Unique glass and crystal cutter's workshop, which looks back on 200 years of history. Here, individual pieces can be restored or authentically reproduced. Owner Paola Locchi will gladly advise you –her ideas are unique. *Via Burchiello 10 | www.locchi.com*

RICHARD GINORI
(130 B3) (*📖 F4*)

The king of Italian porcelain since 1735, every piece made by hand. Good, affordable INSIDER TIP ▶ sales outlet in Sesto Fiorentino (133 D2) (*📖 D5*) (*Viale Giulio Cesare 19*). *Via Rondinelli 17r | www.richardginori1735.com*

JEWELLERY & WATCHES

APROSIO & CO.
(130 B3) (*📖 F5*)

Imaginative pieces crafted from Venetian glass beads and crystals in the shape of flowers, animals, coral, fruits... *Via del Moro 75 | www.aprosio.it*

ENRICO VERITÀ
(130 C3–4) (*📖 F5*)

There are only eight traditional watchmakers left in Italy. In this atelier, you have the feeling you've travelled back in time. Repairs are also carried out. *Via de' Calzaiuoli 122r*

EVEN BIJOUX (131 D4) *(⊞ F5)*
Hand-crafted jewellery according to old and new designs. *Via Dante Alighieri 8r | www.evenbijouxbh.com*

LEATHER GOODS

IL BISONTE ★ ⓢ (130 A4) *(⊞ E5)*
Do you need a new suitcase, handbag or perhaps simply a fine purse or wallet? Elegant luggage, mostly made of naturally tanned cowhide or buffalo hide. *Via del Parione 31r | www.ilbisonte.net*

MARTELLI (131 C5) *(⊞ F5)*
Hand-made gloves, in all styles and colours. *Via Por Santa Maria 18r | www.martelligloves.it*

PELLETTERIA ARTIGIANA VIVIANI
(133 E5) *(⊞ F4)*
The Viviani family has been making leather goods for three generations. Every piece is handcrafted. Here, you can watch Vivaina and her son Leonardo working away at their workshop. *Via Guelfa 3b | www.pelletteriaartigiana.com*

INSIDER TIP **SCUOLA DEL CUOIO**
(131 F5) *(⊞ G5)*
To the left of Santa Croce church, a door leads to the former dormitories of the monastery where the world-famous school of leatherworking is located. Here, you can buy the finest leather goods – bags, jewellery boxes or purses – and have them embossed in gold with your name or initials. *Piazza di Santa Croce 16 | www.leatherschool.biz*

MARBLE

RAFFAELLO ROMANELLI (136 C2) *(⊞ D5)*
Do you fancy your own copy of Michelangelo's *David* for the garden? The 1 : 1 marble reproduction is to be had for 140,000 euros. If your budget won't stretch to that, there are more affordable items (from 4 euros) in marble and stone, too. *Borgo San Frediano 70 | www.raffaelloromanelli.com*

MARKETS

The main weekly market selling fruit, vegetables and many everyday objects

LOW BUDGET

The flea markets on the *Piazza Santo Spirito* (130 A5–6) *(⊞ E6)* every second Sunday or around the large fountains of the *Fortezza da Basso* (133 D–E4) *(⊞ E–F3)* every third Sunday in the month are ideal for bargain-hunting.

The outlets round about Florence are popular destinations: *The Mall* (141 F4) *(⊞ 0)* (daily 10am–7pm | Via Europa 8 | Leccio/Reggello | bus trips almost hourly from Santa Maria Novella for 13 euros/person return | info: tel. 05 58 65 77 75 | www.themall.it)* focuses on brand names such as *Gucci, Dolce & Gabbana, Tod's, Armani, Ferragamo, Fendi, Valentino.* The *Barberino Designer Outlet (daily 10am–8pm | Barberino di Mugello | Scopicci | shuttle service near main railway station Fortezza da Basso (Viale Strozzi | Piazzale Montelungo) 9.30am, 11.30am, 2pm and 4pm, approx. 40 min., return journey from outlet daily 1pm, 3pm, 6pm and 8pm | return ticket 13 euros | info: tel. 0 55 84 21 61 | www.mcarthurglen.it/barberino),* 30 km/18.5 miles to the north, is laid out like a small village, with over 90 international brands.

takes place every Tuesday morning in the *Parco delle Cascine* (132 B5) (*𝄞 B–C 3–4*).

MERCATO CENTRALE ★ ●
(130 B–C1) (*𝄞 F4*)

The large market hall, built in 1784, is an eldorado for lovers of fine foods. Check out the mouth-watering stalls full of local produce and work up an appetite for dinner! *Mon–Sat 7am–3pm; in winter: Sat until 5pm | Via dell'Ariento 10–14 | Piazza del Mercato Centrale*

MERCATO DEL PORCELLINO
(130 C4) (*𝄞 F5*)

Leather goods, ties, fabrics and souvenirs in the *Loggia del Mercato Nuovo* right next to the bronze *porcellino,* whose snout is all shiny because everyone strokes it. Legend has it that you'll return to Florence if you place a coin on his tongue and it falls into the fountain right away. *Tue–Sat 8am–7pm | Via Por Santa Maria*

MERCATO SAN LORENZO ★
(130 B–C 1–2) (*𝄞 F4*)

Fashion items, but also gifts, ceramics and knitwear on this large and very touristy market skirting the church of San Lorenzo and on the adjacent Via dell'Ariento.

A stroll across the market is always fun, especially if you're on the lookout for a souvenir to take home with you. *Tue–Sat 8am–7pm | Piazza San Lorenzo*

INSIDER TIP ► MERCATO DI SANT'AMBROGIO
(138 B2) (*𝄞 H5*)

Come here to experience the most authentic market atmosphere in Florence. For one thing, there are hardly any tourists, and the stallholders know their local customers by name, swapping recipes and looking forward to their certain return the next day. *Mon–Sat 7am–2pm, Wed/Thu until 7.30pm | Piazza Ghiberti*

SHOES

MARIO BEMER
(130 A6) (*𝄞 E6*)

Mario Bemer's workshop is full of made-to-order men's shoes in shining, brightly coloured models. He designs and makes his luxury products here and welcomes any interested onlookers to watch him while working. Not within everyone's price range but a pair of his shoes will last you a lifetime. *Via Maggio 68 | www.mariobemer.com*

MADE TO MEASURE

Treat yourself to the luxury of some bespoke garments or footwear; only here in Florence are these crafts practised to such a professional degree. *Antonio Liverano* (130 A3) (*𝄞 E5*) (*Via dei Fossi 43r | tel. 05 52 39 64 36 | www.liverano.com)* makes classical outfits for you; young shoe expert *Saskia Wittmer* (137 D1) (*𝄞 E4*) (*Via di S. Lucia 24r | tel. 0 55 29 32 91 | www.saskiascarpesumi sura.com)* uses a model of your foot to make the shoe of your dreams and the "world-famous nose" belonging to *Lorenzo Villoresi* (130 C6) (*𝄞 F6*) (*Via dei Bardi 12 | tel. 05 52 34 11 87 | www.lorenzovilloresi.it)* can create the perfum that suits you best. And while you're here, take a little journey through the senses and visit his new "Museum of Frangrances".

Ever wanted to own your own pair of bespoke shoes? Go to Saskia Wittmer!

MONTI CALZATURE (131 D3) (*🕮 F4*)
If all you need is a comfortable pair of shoes, Monti is sure to have something for you. Also Birkenstock sandals and Dr. Scholl's products. Directly behind the cathedral. *Piazza Duomo 27r*

SALVATORE FERRAGAMO
(130 B4) (*🕮 F5*)
The "King of shoemakers" died in 1960, but his acclaimed brand name lives on. Ladies' shoes, accessories and the *Museo Salvatore Ferragamo* (see p. 36). *Via Tornabuoni 16r | www.salvatoreferragamo.it*

UNDERWEAR & LINEN

FERRINI (130 C4) (*🕮 F5*)
High-quality bed- and table linen, nightwear and much more besides. *Via Calimala 5r | www.ferrinifirenze.it*

LORETTA CAPONI ★ (130 B3) (*🕮 F5*)
Loretta began learning embroidery at the age of nine. Today, her atelier and showrooms are located in a 650-m² (780-yd²) Renaissance palace, where she still advises her clients, from Florentine high society and among the crowned heads of Europe. *Piazza Antinori 4r | www.lorettacaponi.com*

WINE

The following dealers have a broad selection of fine Tuscan wines:

ENOTECA ALESSI (139 C3) (*🕮 F5*)
(*Via delle Oche 27r | www.enotecaalessi.com*)

ENOTECA BONATTI (138 C2) (*🕮 J5*)
(*Via Gioberti 68r | www.enotecabonatti.it*)

ENOTECA FIORENTINA
(138 B2) (*🕮 H5*)
(*Via Pietrapiana 11r | enotecafiorentina.it*))

ENTERTAINMENT

CITY **WHERE TO START?**
In the evenings, head for the opposite bank of the Arno to the quarters of **San Niccolò (138 A4)** *(ℳ F–G6)* and **Santo Spirito (137 D–E3)** *(ℳ E–F 5–6)*. Cool bars have also sprung up in the small alleyways around **Santa Croce (131 E–F5)** *(ℳ G5)*. Around 7pm, people meet up for happy hour to take an aperitif and to eat from opulent buffets, usually at a fixed price. There are also several clubs for later on, but most clubs are located on the outskirts of the city and can only be reached by car or taxi.

If a stroll through the streets and alleyways of the nocturnal city centre is not your idea of a good night out – although it's a fascinating experience in itself – Florence has plenty of options for an eventful and varied evening. And that's without having a true entertainment district of its own.

The centre has loads of trendy bars and jazz clubs, whereas most discos are on the periphery. The Florentine theatre scene is particularly lively. The 200 or so performances per year are often guest appearances and represent a good cross-section of Italian theatre in general. Advance ticket sales: *Box Office (Via delle Vecchie Carceri 1 | tel. 0 55 21 08 0 | www. boxofficetoscana.it)*

Whether bar, disco, open-air concert or a dose of culture at the theatre or opera – Florentine nights are anything but boring

CONCERTS

AUDITORIUM FLOG
(141 E2) (*Ø O*)

Lots of live concerts, mostly pop and rock, but also reggae, hip-hop and blues. Thursday, Friday and Saturday parties with good DJs. At 5–30 euros, admission prices are reasonable. Open-air cinema in summer. *Oct–May | Via Michele Mercati 24b | tel. 0 55 47 79 78 | www.flog.it*

MANDELA FORUM
(135 E5) (*Ø K4*)

Largest events venue in the city: Sporting events and concerts from national and international musicians and stars. *Piazza Berlinguer | tel. 0 55 67 88 41 | www.mandelaforum.it*

OBIHALL (141 E3) (*Ø M6*)

The Florentine equivalent of the London Arena with the latest line-up of concerts and shows. *Lungarno Aldo Moro 3 | tel. 05 56 50 41 12 | www.obihall.it*

TEATRO DELLA PERGOLA ⭐

(131 E3) (📖 G4)

Historical theatre dating back to 1755, in which chamber concerts and plays are staged. *Via della Pergola 18 | tel. 05 52 26 43 53 | www.teatrodellapergola. com*

TEATRO VERDI ⭐ (131 E4) (📖 G5)

Situated in the Santa Croce neighbourhood, this large, old Italian-style theatre hosts shows from every genre, ranging from classic to pop. *Via Ghibellina 99 | tel. 0 55 212 32 0 | www.teatroverdifirenze.it, www.orchestradellatoscana.it*

DISCOTHEQUES

Opening times can vary according to the time of year. It might be a good idea to ring up first! Admission prices are usually around 25 euros.

DOLCE ZUCCHERO (131 E4) (📖 G5)

Much-loved disco-pub, especially popular with young tourists and students on the European Erasmus Programme. Separate room for live music. *Australian Beach Bar* with separate entrance to have a chat with more subduesd music. *Daily 10pm–4am | Via Pandolfini 36r*

FULL UP (132 D4) (📖 G5)

Since the 1970s, a nightlife favourite. One of few clubs with a smoking zone. *Thu–Sat and Mon from 11pm | Via della Vigna Vecchia 23 | www.fullupclub.com*

OTEL ⭐ (141 E3) (📖 O)

Mix of disco and cabaret: Start with a meal accompanied by a show and cabaret from 8.30pm before hitting the dancefloor with a good DJ set from 11.30pm. *Mid-Sept–mid-May Fri–Sun | Viale Generale dalla Chiesa 9 | www.otelvariete.com*

Aperitif or a last one for the road: Zoe

OPERA DI FIRENZE ⭐

(132 C5) (📖 D4)

Since 2014, performances of *Maggio Musicale Fiorentino* – the oldest and most famous music festival in Italy – are held in the new avant-garde building *Nuovo Teatro dell'Opera*. A breath-taking view of the city can be had from the connected ☀ *Open-Air Auditorium*. Outside the main festival season (Jan–April and Sept–Dec), the theatre offers a diverse program of concerts, operas and ballets. *Viale Fratelli Rosselli 1 | www.operadifirenze.it*

SPACE (133 D6) *(ⅲ E4)*
Located at the heart of the city, a popular haunt for young Florentine locals to dance to house, hip-hop and happy music/revival. *Daily from 10pm | Via Palazzuolo 37*

TENAX ⭐ (141 D2)
This disco near the airport is a household name all over Italy. International DJs and a different programme every day. *Oct–May Fri/Sat from 10pm | Via Pratese 46 | www.tenax.org*

YAB ⭐ (130 C4) *(ⅲ F5)*
The absolute *über*-disco right in the centre of Florence. Aperitif, evening meal and live music all rolled into one. *Daily from 9.30pm | Via dei Sassetti 5r | tel. 055215160 | www.yab.it*

ROOFTOP BARS

You don't have to be an overnight guest to enter most of the city's exclusive hotel bars. Simply put your glad rags on and take the lift up to the top floor: besides the amazing cityscape views, there are other delights waiting to take your breath away. Some of the larger hotels serve not only cocktails and snacks or lunch and dinner on their rooftop terrace, they even have a pool – which is lit up at night! Some of the recommended ⭐ ⋇ *rooftop bars* include: *Se.Sto on Arno, Westin Excelsior* (137 D2) *(ⅲ E5) (Piazza Ognissanti 3 | www.sestoonarno.com), Empireo, Plaza Hotel Lucchesi* (138 B3) *(ⅲ H6) (Piazza Ognissanti 3 | hotelplazalucchesi.it), Grand Hotel Minerva* (130 A2) *(ⅲ E4) (Piazza Santa Maria Novella 16 | www.grandhotelminerva.com)* and *Hotel Baglioni* (130 B2) *(ⅲ F4) (Piazza Unità Italiana 6 | www.hotelbaglioni.it)*

THEATRE

Florentines spend more money on the theatre than any of their compatriots. Alongside traditional theatres, many small companies have established them-

---

⭐ **Dolce Vita**
The cocktails go down well not only during happy hour → p. 87

⭐ **Tabasco**
Where boys will be boys → p. 89

⭐ **Moyo**
Chill-out lounge for young people → p. 88

⭐ **Otel**
Popular destination for local disco fans → p. 84

⭐ **Rooftop bars**
Enjoy your aperitif over the rooftops of Florence → p. 85

⭐ **Tenax**
Top international DJs set Tenax buzzing with music from minimal via techno to house → p. 85

⭐ **Yab**
Disco must in the centre is also a good place for dinner → p. 85

⭐ **Opera di Firenze**
Main stage for concerts, opera and ballet of the Maggio Musicale → p. 84

⭐ **Teatro Verdi**
A theatre with a very young cast and contemporary program → p. 84

⭐ **Teatro della Pergola**
Top-flight ensembles make for unforgettable evenings of music and drama in a historic setting → p. 84

MARCO POLO HIGHLIGHTS

selves in the city, from chamber theatre to experimental drama – in summer, also in the gardens and courtyards of palaces and monasteries. Performances during the *Estate Fiesolana* (see p. 114), which usually take place in the *Teatro Romano*, the Roman theatre in Fiesole, are highly impressive.

Find the current programs in the daily newspapers La Nazione *(www.lanazione. it)* and La Repubblica *(www.repubblica.it)*.

EX-STAZIONE LEOPOLDA
(132 C5) (*ш D3–4*)

Since the mid-1990s, the huge halls of the former station have been the loca-tion for exhibitions, diverse happenings and performances and also the interna-tional theatre festival which takes place in May. *Viale Fratelli Rosselli 5 | www. stazione-leopolda.com*

INSIDER TIP ODEON CINEHALL
(130 B4) (*ш F5*)

A delight for cinemagoers – even those who do not understand Italian – as every day, films are screened here in the original language. Not only can you enjoy the film, but the surroundings are a treat, too: a beautiful film palace with a magical 1920s interior. An experience you'd be hard put to repeat anywhere else these days. *Piazza Strozzi 2 | tel. 0 55 29 50 51 | www.cinehall.it*

TEATRO DELLA LIMONAIA (141 E2)

They've been playing avant-garde thea-tre in the suburb of Sesto Fiorentino since 1987. Performances take place in the el-egant orangery of the Villa Corsi Salviati. *Via Gramsci 426 | tel. 0 55 44 08 52 | www. teatrodellalimonaia.it*

TEATRO PUCCINI (141 D3) (*ш B2*)

Highly popular with local residents, this venue offers a colourful programme, ranging from satirical cabaret to musi-cals. *Via delle Cascine 41/Piazza Puccini | tel. 0 55 36 20 67 | www.teatropuccini.it*

INSIDER TIP TEATRO DEL SALE
(130 B2) (*ш H5*)

A theatre and, at the same time, a res-taurant and delicatessen: Once you've purchased your membership card for 11 euros at the door, you can brunch, lunch or dine in these evocative surroundings, seated in leather armchairs, surrounded by old bookcases or in full view of the kitchen. In the evening, you can even experience the king of Florentine cuisine, Fabio Picchi, as he himself serves you your

LOW BUDGET

In many bars during happy hour from around 7pm you can enjoy an *aperi-tivo* and get a bite to eat from the buffet – almost for free: small snacks, pasta salads, rice dishes, salads and lots more besides. The "banquets" are particularly sumptuous at *Kitsch 1* **(138 C2)** (*ш G3*) *(daily 6.30pm–3am | Vile Gramsci 1–5 | www.kitschfirenze. com)* or at *Plaz* **(131 F4)** (*ш H5*) *(dai-ly aperitif from 6.30pm–10pm | Via Pietrapiana 26r)* on the pretty Piazza de' Ciompi, a safe bet from breakfast right through to nightcap time.

Unfortunately by no means the norm in Florentine discos: You can get in the popular *Twice Club* **(131 E5)** (*ш G5*) *(daily from 7pm | Via Verdi 57r | www. twiceclub.com)* for free. Atmosphere and music are unbeatable!

Wednesday is film day; admission is only 6.50 euros.

The Teatro del Sale is a marriage of culinary and dramatic art

food (it is wise to be there from around 7pm!). Sometimes it's so cramped on the tiny benches that you can't even put your glass down. Shortly before 9pm, the tables are pushed together, and the performance begins. More information about the current programme on the Internet. Even without a show, an evening here is sure to be an unforgettable experience. *Tue–Sat 9am–10.30am, Sun 9am–2.30pm | brunch: 7 euros; lunch: 20 euros; dinner: 30 euros | Via dei Macci 111r | tel. 05 52 00 14 92 | www.teatrodelsale.com*

TEATRO DI RIFREDI (141 E3)

Musicals and experimental theatre, performed in the suburb of Rifredi. *Via Vittorio Emanuele II 303 | tel. 05 54 22 03 61 | www.toscanateatro.it*

TRENDY BARS & PUBS

BITTER BAR (138 B2) (*ℳ H5*)

A great place to shake up your cocktail repertoire with a laid-back atmosphere, good music and sophisticated drinks in the Sant'Ambrogio district. *Daily from 7pm | Via di Mezzo 28r | www.bitterbar firenze.it*

DOLCE VITA ★ (137 D2) (*ℳ E5*)

See and be seen: First-rate cocktails are mixed during *happy hour* from 5pm, then the place is packed to the gills until 3am. Disco-bar with small exhibitions and mini-concerts – for 20 years now! Outside, too, in summer. *Tue–Sun 9am–3am | Piazza del Carmine 6r | www.dolce vitaflorence.com*

FLÒ ☽ (138 B4) (*ℳ H6*)

Live music, DJ set, glamour, aperitif buffet and – from a southern hilltop – an amazing view over Florence! *Daily 8pm–4am | Piazzale Michelangelo 84 | www.flo firenze.com*

HEMINGWAY (137 D3) (*ℳ E5*)

An absolute *must* for chocolate junkies! They also have good, home-made ice cream, cake (unlike much of what you'll get elsewhere in Florence!), many varieties of tea and coffee, crêpes etc. *Tue–Sun from 5pm | Piazza Piattellina 9r | www.hemingway.fi.it*

JAZZ CLUB FIRENZE (131 F3) *(𝄞 G4)*
Fans flock to their favourite venue from 11pm, on Tue and Thu also for the jam session. From June to September, the whole set-up moves to the park at the *Villa Fabbricotti (130 A3) (𝄞 F1) (Tue–Sat | Via Vittorio Emanuele). From 11pm | admission approx. 8 euros | Via Nuova de' Caccini 3/Borgo Pinti*

MAD SOUL & SPIRITS (137 D3) *(𝄞 E5)*
In Florence's coolest and cult neighbourhood, San Frediano, alchemists Neri and Julian attract a discerning crowd with their excellent and contemporary cocktail creations. The party goes on well into the early hours of the morning. *Daily 6pm–2am | Borgo San Frediano 36r*

MOYO ⭐
(131 E5) *(𝄞 G5)*
The agenda at this cult hang-out near Santa Croce: from 8am till 3pm, a chat over breakfast; a little discussion over lunch; after the aperitif a bit of flirting till the small hours. *Daily 8am–3am | Via dei Benci 23r | www.moyo.it*

REX CAFFÈ (131 F3) *(𝄞 G5)*
American bar on an ocean liner in the middle of the city: good combination of colourful cocktails, fresh snacks and, after 10 pm, live music. *Sept–mid-May daily 6pm–2.30am | Via Fiesolana 23r | www.rexfirenze.com*

INSIDER TIP ▶ IL RIFRULLO
(138 A4) *(𝄞 G6)*
Inside, cosy atmosphere in front of the open fire; outside, romantic roof terrace. Here, you can really have a good time, from the first cappuccino of the day to a glass of good wine or a fruity cocktail late

FOR BOOKWORMS & FILM BUFFS

A Room With A View – Romantic: James Ivory's film account of the love story between well-bred Miss Honeychurch and the eccentric, but very appealing young man George at the turn of the century was awarded three Oscars and filmed at several locations in Florence, such as the Piazza della Signoria and the Fattoria di Maiano (1986)

Tea with Mussolini – Full of caustic humour: Franco Zeffirelli made this autobiographical tragicomedy about the fate of English "Florentines" at the end of the war. Backdrop was the city centre, the surrounding hills and San Gimignano (1999)

Inferno – Nerve-racking action thriller: The third instalment in the series of Dan Brown films about the symbology professor and researcher from Harvard, Robert Langdon, played by Tom Hanks. Most of the scenes were filmed in Florence (2016)

Hannibal – The fact that the eloquent cannibal Hannibal Lecter from Thomas Harris' novels turns up again in Florence of all places (and as a museum curator!) was a not insignificant factor in the great success of Ridley Scott's thriller (2001)

Ballet, theatre, opera, pop & jazz – something for everyone at the historic Teatro Verdi

at night. *Daily 7.30am–130am | Via San Niccolò 55r | www.ilrifrullo.com*

TABASCO ⭐ (130 C4) (*𝄞 F5*)
Cocktail bar for men only near the Piazza della Signoria. Till 4 in the morning, this is the heart of the city's homosexual scene. Thu–Sat also disco until 6am. *Piazza di Santa Cecilia 3*

VANILLA CLUB (131 D5) (*𝄞 G5–6*)
The perfect place if you like jazz and the 1930s. This speak-easy cocktail bar is hidden away in a small lane close to the Uffizi. You need an annual club card to get in – but at only 5 euros, it's well worth it and you can come back time and time again during your stay. *Daily 6pm–2am | Via dei Saponai 14r | www.vanillaclub.it*

VOLUME (130 A6) (*𝄞 E6*)
Bini's old cabinet-maker's workshop has been transformed into a bar with cult status. Against a 1970s backdrop, you can read, eat excellent crêpes, listen to live music or simply have a drink. *Mon–Wed 4.30pm–1am, Thu–Sun 8.30am–1.30am | Piazza Santo Spirito 5r | www.volume.fi.it*

ZOE (138 A4) (*𝄞 G6*)
Popular watering hole, also good for a quick lunch with the young working population of San Niccolò; it also suits the upper-class student fraternity, who get together here for an aperitif. *Daily 8.30am–2am | Via dei Renai 13r | www.zoebar.it*

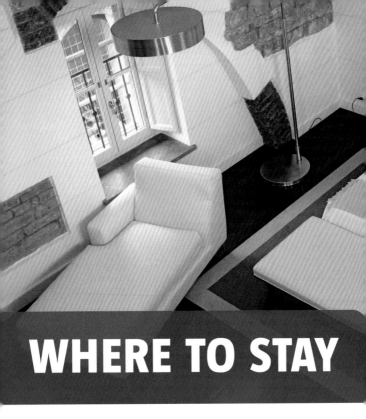

WHERE TO STAY

Regardless of whether you're planning a short city break and need a centrally located hotel or an extended stay in the countryside overlooking the city – the key to any Florence trip is to book early! Are you bringing your family with you to Florence? If so, you'll find plenty of information at *Italy Family Hotels (tel. 05 41 39 48 51 | www.italyfamilyhotels. com)*. Details of good, value-for-money accommodation can be had from *Apartments in Florence (tel. 0 55 36 21 81 | www. apartmentsinflorence.net)*. The *Consorzio Informazioni Turistiche Alberghiere (www. firenzealbergo.it)* carries out free hotel reservations. The brochure entitled *Guida all'ospitalità,* containing information on all accommodation in Florence and the surrounding area, is available free of charge from the tourist information office *(www.firenzeturismo.it)*.

In 2011, the city of Florence has established a visitor's tax for overnight stays (up to seven consecutive nights) of 1–5 euros per night, depending on the category of the hotel. Children under 12 are exempt.

HOTELS: EXPENSIVE

BRUNELLESCHI (131 D4) *(ſ F5)*
Spend the night in one of the oldest buildings in the city, with its tower from the Byzantine era. Modern and luxuriously furnished, with a good restaurant and located in the heart of the city. *96 rooms | Piazza Santa Elisabetta 3 | tel. 05 52 73 70 | www.hotelbrunelleschi.it*

Photo: Gallery Hotel Art

Would you prefer to bed down in a historical city palace, designer hotel, a B & B or a family-sized villa out in the sticks?

EXECUTIVE (133 D6) *(ꄲ D4)*
Elegant hotel centrally located on the Arno. Some rooms even have their own private sauna. Car parking at extra cost. *48 rooms | Via Curtatone 5 | tel. 0 55 21 74 51 | www.hotelexecutive.it*

GALLERY HOTEL ART ★
(130 C5) *(ꄲ F5)*
Cool hotel that will appeal to anyone into Japanese minimalism. There are no frills in this establishment. The hotel's *Fusion Bar* serves delicious food and cocktails. Tucked away on a surprisingly quiet piazza and just a few steps from the Ponte Vecchio, this hotel is about as central as you can get. *74 rooms* INSIDER TIP *(nos. 701, 707 and 708 with roof terrace!) | Vicolo dell'Oro 5 | tel. 0 55 27 26 40 00 | www.lungarnocollection.com/gallery-hotel-art*

GRAND HOTEL MINERVA
(130 A2–3) *(ꄲ E4)*
Central location, quiet rooms at the rear. Warm, welcoming service and a beautiful

Sensational, breath-taking views from the Palazzo Guadagni loggia

swimming pool on the roof. Incidentally, even if you're not staying at the hotel, you can enjoy an aperitif at the substantial buffet by the pool on Thursdays INSIDER TIP at *Minerva Giò,* including live music, for just 15 euros *(mid-May–early Aug 7.30pm–10pm)*! *110 rooms | Piazza Santa Maria Novella 16 | tel. 05 52 72 30 | www.grandhotelminerva.com*

HH FLORENCE (138 B3) (*H6*)

Pure, unadulterated luxury, not just for honeymooners. At this "Hotel Home", everything – tables, chairs, floors, beds – is dazzling white, with a touch of gold here and there. Large panorama terrace. *39 rooms | Piazza Piave 3 | tel. 0 55 24 36 68 | www.hhflorence.it*

JK PLACE (130 A3) (*E4*)

A very elegant, intimate hotel, oozing with charm and style on the spacious Piazza Santa Maria Novella. View of the town from the 🌿 roof terrace. *20 rooms | Piazza Santa Maria Novella 7 | tel. 05 52 64 51 81 | www.jkplace.com*

LUNGARNO ⭐ 🌿 (130 B5) (*F5*)

Modern, luxurious, on the southern bank of the Arno only 100 m/328 ft from the Ponte Vecchio. On the premises: excellent restaurant *Borgo San Jacopo (closed Aug | Moderate–Expensive). 65 rooms | Borgo Sant'Jacopo 14 | tel. 0 55 27 26 40 00 | www.lungarnohotels.com*

PALAZZO GUADAGNI ⭐
(130 A6) (*E6*)

Overlooking the Santo Spirito Piazza and the Palazzo Pitti, the loggia terrace of this romantic hotel is fantastic and the ideal place for a relaxing evening drink. In true grandeur style, the hotel features antique furniture, high ceilings with frescoes and stucco creating a stylish ambience. It has an ample breakfast buffet and the rooms are spacious; room no. 1 is splendid even if the small balcony is above the lively, and loud, piazza below. However, there are rooms at the back overlooking the courtyard. *15 rooms | Piazza Santo Spirito 9 | tel. 05 52 65 83 76 | www.palazzoguadagni.com*

TORRE DI BELLOSGUARDO ★ ⬳
(136 B4) *(𝄞 C6)*
Tranquillity and hospitality in a fine Renaissance villa, overlooking the city from the south. Spacious park with pool. *16 rooms | Via Roti Michelozzi 2 | tel. 05 52 29 81 45 | www.torrebellosguardo.com*

VILLA CARLOTTA ★ **(127 D5)** *(𝄞 E7)*
Elegant yet welcoming atmosphere in a 19th-century villa on the green slopes above the Porta Romana and the Boboli Gardens. With own car park and pool. *33 rooms | Via Michele di Lando 3 | tel. 0 55 22 05 30 | www.hotelvillacarlotta.it*

HOTELS: MODERATE

ANNALENA ★ **(137 D4)** *(𝄞 E6)*
Romantic boutique hotel in a prime location near the Boboli Gardens. The prettiest rooms lead off the open gallery and have views onto the hotel garden. *20 rooms | Via Romana 34 | tel. 0 55 22 24 02 | www.annalenahotel.com*

BENCISTÀ ★ ⬳ **(141 E3)** *(𝄞 N2)*
This stylish family hotel is located halfway to Fiesole, on a hillside amidst olive groves. Friendly atmosphere and a fabulous view over the city. 6 km (4 miles) from the city centre. *40 rooms | March–Nov | Via Benedetto da Maiano 4 | Fiesole | tel. 05 59 91 63 | www.bencista.com*

MORANDI ALLA CROCETTA ★
(131 F1) *(𝄞 G4)*
Small, stylish, relatively quiet hotel in a former monastery, close to SS. Anunziata. Ideal for families. Garage at extra cost. *10 rooms | Via Laura 50 | tel. 05 52 34 47 47 | www.hotelmorandi.it*

INSIDER TIP ORTO DEI MEDICI
(133 F5) *(𝄞 G3)*
Pleasant hotel in the centre, with pretty rooms, car park and a delightful garden where Lorenzo de'Medici founded his sculpture school. *42 rooms | Via San Gallo 30 | tel. 0 55 48 34 27 | www.orto deimedici.it*

★ **Gallery Hotel Art** Fine hotel in great location; sometimes transformed into a gallery → p. 91

★ **Lungarno** Modern and tasteful, right by the Ponte Vecchio → p. 92

★ **Torre di Bellosguardo** Renaissance villa with pool, park and panoramic view over the city → p. 93

★ **Villa Carlotta** Charming country-house flair, close to the centre → p. 93

★ **Annalena** Bijou domicile near the Boboli Gardens → p. 93

★ **Palazzo Guadagni** Hotel for nostalgics → p. 92

★ **Bencistà** Villa with an informal touch in the hills of Fiesole → p. 93

★ **Villa Agape** Hotel surrounded by greenery with shuttle service → p. 96

★ **Morandi alla Crocetta** Stylish, charming and, believe it or not, affordable → p. 93

★ **Fattoria di Maiano** Holiday between art and olives, on the premises of a former monastery → p. 97

MARCO POLO HIGHLIGHTS

PALAZZO DEL BORGO
(133 D6) (*m E4*)

Spell-bounding hotel, tastefully decorated with a delightful garden in the historic Palazzo del Borgo. It's also centrally located. *34 rooms | Via della Scala 6 | tel. 0 55 21 62 37 | www.hotelpalazzodalbo rgo.it*

INSIDER TIP RESIDENCE LA MEDICEA ☆ (130 C2) (*m F4*)

Individual, tastefully-designed mini apartments (for 2–5 people) in the heart of the city with an amazing view of the Cappelle Medicee dome within reach. Minimum 3-night stay. *11 flats | Via dell'Ariento 3r | mobile phone*

MORE THAN A GOOD NIGHT'S SLEEP

Well protected in Morpheus' arms

Where today can you sleep in a four-poster bed under a canopy? The romantic *Loggiato dei Serv_ti* (131 E1) (*m G4*) (*38 rooms | Piazza Santissima Annunziata 3 | tel. 0 55 28 95 92 | www.loggiato deiservitihotel.it | Moderate–Expensive*) is filled with splendid antique furniture and pictures and a wonderful collection of beds to choose from. Some of the rooms have small balconies overlooking the delightful Piazza Santissima Annunziata. The hotel is casually elegant and you would never guess that it was once a guesthouse run by the monks of the Servite Order.

Floating Gods and restless spirits – all inclusive

If the thought of being kissed good-night by a good-looking stranger sounds a little creepy to you, don't book a night in room no. 5 at the *Burchianti* (130 B2) (*m F4*) (*11 rooms | Via del Giglio 8 | tel. 0 55 21 27 96 | www.hotel burchianti.it | Budget*) A tidy chambermaid from old times in need of love is said to haunt this room, performing her spooky shenanigans on sleeping guests. She sounds scary but, in fact, she has been banned to the ceiling's fresco for centuries. Many of the paintings and frescoes in the rooms offer lessons in Greek mythology – that's if you are finding it difficult to fall asleep.

Florence in the treetops

Have you ever slept in a treehouse? The *Tree House Casa Barthel* (141 D3) (*m 0*) (*1 room | Via Volterrana 103 | mobile tel. 33 55 71 17 86 | www.casabarthel.com | Moderate*) offers contemporary tree-houses to accommodate two people for visitors to get up close to nature and enjoy a unique experience. The tranquil setting is the perfect place to relax and recover from all the sightseeing and hustle and bustle in the city. The large ☆ garden with pool offers spectacular views over the city.

Old England atmosphere

A last outpost of the British colonies in Florence is the *Helvetia & Bristol* (130 B3) (*m F5*) (*67 rooms | Via dei Pescioni 2 | tel. 05 52 66 51 | www.star hotelcollezione.com | Expensive*) with splendid dining room and exquisite restaurant, nostalgic conservatory for tea-time as well as contemporary decorated rooms. This historic hotel has a super-central location just a few steps from the Cathedral and shopping mile, but also tucked away in a quiet side street.

Don't want a chain hotel? Then stay at the super-central Tornabuoni Beacci

33 58 11 66 88 | www.residencelamedicea. com

INSIDER TIP HOTEL ROYAL
(133 F4) (*∅ F3*)
Situated in a 19th-century villa, with a large garden and pool. Quiet and yet not far from the station. *39 rooms | Via delle Ruote 50–54 | tel. 0 55 48 32 87 | www. hotelroyalfirenze.it*

TORNABUONI BEACCI (130 B4) (*∅ F5*)
This small hotel is full of cosy charm where guests can feel at home. The public areas and rooms recall genteel "Room with a View" days and the view from the cosy ☼ terrace is simply fantastic. Located on the city's most exclusive shopping street, this tastefully furnished hotel is opposite Ferragamo and just a few metres from the banks of the Arno. *56 rooms | Via Torna-buoni 3 | tel. 0 55 21 26 45 | www.torna buonihotels.com*

HOTELS: BUDGET

ALESSANDRA ☼ (130 B5) (*∅ F5*)
Hotel with large rooms; numbers 21, 22 and 26 also have a view of the Arno. *27 rooms | closed mid-Dec and mid-Aug | Borgo Santi Apostoli 17 | tel. 0 55 28 34 38 | www.hotelalessandra. com*

ARIZONA (138 B2) (*∅ H4*)
Just a few steps from the bustling Sant'Ambrogio weekly market with cosy rooms and, for Italian standards, ample breakfast. *21 rooms | Via Farini 2 | tel. 0 55 24 53 21 | www.arizonahotel.it*

ORCAGNA (138–139 C–D3) (*∅ J5*)
The perfect place for a short city break in Florence: slightly away from the tourist crowds but still in a central location. The rooms are spacious, clean and contemporarily furnished and you can spot the cathedral's dome from the ☼ rooftop

terrace. *17 rooms | Via Orcagna 57/59 | tel. 0 55 66 99 59 | www.hotelorcagna firenze.it*

OSTELLO TASSO (136 C3) *(∅ D6)*

Although listed as one of the city's better hostels, this establishment could easily be rated as a boutique hotel. There are simple six-bed dorms available as well as chic single and double rooms. The

Immaculately polished: brass sign of the Hotel La Scaletta

common rooms are designed in a modern vintage style and events are often held here in the evenings. Situated away from the crowds of tourists. *13 rooms | Via Villani 15 | tel. 05 50 60 20 87 | www. tassohostelflorence.com*

ROOM MATE LUCCA (133 F3) *(∅ F3)*

Ideal for partygoers, young couples or friends: Breakfast is served until 12 noon at this laid-back hotel. Large rooms with playful yet stylish decor. *53 rooms | Via XXVII Aprile 3 | tel. 05 52 64 55 39 | www. room-matehotels.com*

HOTEL LA SCALETTA (130 B6) *(∅ F6)*

The rooms are pleasantly cool in summer, and there's a roof terrace for romantic dinners! Friendly service. Near the Ponte Vecchio. *15 rooms | Via Guicciardini 13 | tel. 0 55 28 30 28 | www.lascaletta.com*

UNGHERESE (135 D4) *(∅ K2)*

Whether its rock, pop or football you're interested in – all venues are just a few minutes on foot from this small hotel dating back to the 19th century. Cosy atmosphere and breakfast served on the terrace in summer *15 rooms | Via G.B. Amici 8 | tel.05 55 73 474 | www.hot elungherese.it*

VILLA AGAPE ★ (137 F6) *(∅ G8)*

Surrounded by a 17-acre park with olive and cypress trees, this hidden jewel stands in a tranquil setting overlooking the city. A free round-trip shuttle service to the city centre is also available. What more could you possibly want? *28 rooms | Via Torre del Gallo 8 | tel. 0 55 22 00 44 | www.villaagape.it*

AGRITURISMO/B & B

B & B ALBERGHINO ⚜
(133 D5) *(∅ E3)*

Antiques lover Letizia takes care of her guests as if they were friends: She gives restaurant tips, helps with ticket reservations and always knows what's going on where. Near the Fortezza di Basso. *5 rooms | Via Cittadella 6a | tel. 05 53 31 42 | www.alberghino.it*

FATTORIA DI MAIANO ★ ☆
(141 E2) (*🕮 0*)

Twelve cosy apartments in the grounds of a 15th-century monastery which has often been used as a film set. Swimming pool. Restaurant which uses ingredients from its own production and a small farm. Bookable only by the week; for two persons, approx. 800 euros. *Via Benedetto da Maiano 11 | Fiesole | tel. 0 55 59 96 00 | www.fattoriadimaiano.com*

FLORENCE OLD BRIDGE
(130 B6) (*🕮 F6*)

Admittedly not the quietest location situated directly on the tourist mile between Ponte Vecchio and Palazzo Pitti, however the hotel offers modern and tastefully furnished rooms. Breakfast is served in the *La Scaletta* Hotel opposite. *6 rooms | Via Guicciardini 22r | tel. 05 52 65 42 62 | www.florenceoldbridge.com*

PALAZZO RUSPOLI (130 C2) (*🕮 F4*)

The ideal residence for a weekend trip or a longer stay. Walk out of the hotel and you're literally on the cathedral square. Inside, this royal hotel has been lavishly renovated with all modern comforts. *20 rooms | Via Martelli 5 | tel. 05 52 67 05 63 | www.palazzo-ruspoli.it*

INSIDER TIP ▶ RELAIS IL CESTELLO
(137 D2) (*🕮 E5*)

On the south bank of the Arno, pretty B & B on a piazzetta, looking out onto the river near Santa Maria del Carmine. Friendly service. *10 rooms | Piazza di Cestello 9 | tel. 0 55 28 06 32 | www.relaisilcestello.it*

RESIDENZA IL CARMINE
(137 D3) (*🕮 E6*)

Six prettily furnished apartments (four give onto the garden courtyard, with sitting area) with bathroom and cooking facilities for 2–4 persons. Ideal also for a longer stay. Quiet, but located in the lively district of Santo Spirito. Minimum stay three nights. *Via d'Ardiglione 28 | tel. 05 52 38 20 60 | www.residenzailcarmine.com*

CAMPING

CAMPING PANORAMICO FIESOLE
☆ (141 E2) (*🕮 0*)

Small quiet campsite, with a view over Florence and a beautiful pool. Free shuttle service to Fiesole. *110 spaces | Mid-March–Oct | Fiesole | Via Peramonda 1 | tel. 0 55 59 90 69 | www.florencecamping.com*

LOW BUDGET

Popular youth hostels are the *Ostello Villa Camerata* **(135 F3)** (*🕮 L1*) (ouble rooms and dorms: 18–30 euros/pers. incl. breakfast | Viale Augusto Righi 2–4 | tel. 0 55 60 14 51 | bus 11, 10 min. from the cathedral)*, out in the country towards Fiesole; the *Ostello Santa Monaca* **(137 D3)** (*🕮 E5*) (dorms 18–25 euros/pers. | Via Santa Monaca 6 | tel. 0 55 26 83 38 | www.ostellosantamonaca.it*) in a former monastery in Oltrarno and the centrally located *Plus Florence* **(133 F4)** (*🕮 F3*) (doubles and dorms 20–30 euros/pers. | Via Santa Caterina D'Alessandria 15 | tel. 05 54 62 89 34 | www.plusflorence.com*) with roof terrace and pool – there's no cooler location at this price!

Reservations and tips for B & Bs: *www.bbplanet.it* and *www.bed-and-breakfast.it.*

DISCOVERY TOURS

---

1 FLORENCE AT A GLANCE

START: **1** Piazza della Signoria
END: **18** Teatro della Pergola

1 day
Walking time
(without stops)
1½ hours

Distance:
➡ 6 km/3.7 miles

COSTS: 4–10 euros per church/museum visit

The city of Florence is one gigantic living work of art. It is impossible to see everything so we recommend concentrating on the landmarks. The best way to really soak up this city's atmosphere is to take a stroll across its vast squares and along its winding narrow streets while enjoying some delicacies – and a lot of art!

Would you like to explore the places that are unique to this city? Then the Discovery Tours are just the thing for you – they include terrific tips for stops worth making, breathtaking places to visit, selected restaurants and fun activities. It's even easier with the Touring App: download the tour with map and route to your smartphone using the QR Code on pages 2/3 or from the website address in the footer below – and you'll never get lost again even when you're offline.

TOURING APP

→ p. 2/3

08:00am The perfect start to the day is at ❶ **Piazza della Signoria** → p. 39 with a brioche and an excellent cappuccino to be taken at the famous **Rivoire** → p. 64 or even try a cup of their delicious hot chocolate which is famous throughout Italy! This vast piazza belongs to one of the most inspiring sights in Florence along with the **Palazzo Vecchio** → p. 38 and the **Loggia dei Lanzi** → p. 34. Now take a stroll along the Via dei Calzaiuoli, take a left at the former granary and church adorned with sculptures ❷ **Orsanmichele** → p. 36, and wander across the

❶ Piazza della Signoria 🚶

❷ Orsanmichele 🏠

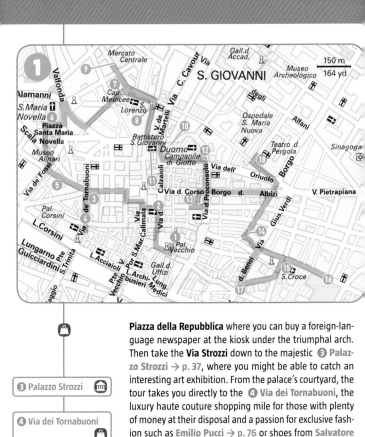

Piazza della Repubblica where you can buy a foreign-language newspaper at the kiosk under the triumphal arch. Then take the **Via Strozzi** down to the majestic ❸ **Palazzo Strozzi → p. 37**, where you might be able to catch an interesting art exhibition. From the palace's courtyard, the tour takes you directly to the ❹ **Via dei Tornabuoni**, the luxury haute couture shopping mile for those with plenty of money at their disposal and a passion for exclusive fashion such as **Emilio Pucci → p. 76** or shoes from **Salvatore Ferragamo → p. 81**.

If you are interested in modern art, then go **along the medieval Via della Spada to the Piazza San Pancrazio** and, in the church which shares the same name, visit the ❺ **Museo Marino Marini → p. 47** with works from this artist who died in 1980. From here you can take a three-minute walk **along the Via della Spada and Via di Fossi** to the beautifully spacious Piazza Santa Maria Novella. Take a seat on one of the benches to read your newspaper or soak up the sun before entering the church ❻ **Santa Maria Novella → p. 48** with its vast store of art treasures including its amazing frescoes.

12:00pm Now the tour takes you further into the city centre **down the Via del Giglio** to an impressive mauso-

❸ Palazzo Strozzi

❹ Via dei Tornabuoni

❺ Museo
Marino Marini

❻ Santa Maria Novella

leum from the House of Medici, the ❼ **Cappelle Medicee** → p. 45 that belongs to the church of **San Lorenzo** → p. 45. You'll find the booming tourist market here in the side streets where you can be sure to spot a nice souvenir. If you've now worked up an appetite, go to ❽ **Gozzi Sergio** → p. 71 opposite the church: you can enjoy a plate of delicious pasta amongst many locals in this authentic trattoria. If you can't get a table, head **100 m/328 ft to your right down the Via dell'Ariento** to the culinary paradise ❾ **Mercato Centrale** → p. 80, where you can put together your own meal from the INSIDER TIP delicious selection of Italian specialties on offer on the first floor of this large market hall. And even if your stomach is full, the building's ground floor is well worth seeing with its vast array of market stalls selling fresh regional specialities.

After a good meal and refreshment, it's now time to walk along the **Borgo San Lorenzo** with its many shoe shops until you reach the square between the towering cathedral ❿ **Duomo di Santa Maria del Fiore** → p. 30 and the ⓫ **Baptistery** → p. 28. Additionally, you should give yourself enough time to look inside the ⓬ **Grande Museo del Duomo** → p. 34 **to the east of the cathedral** containing original works of the fascinating sculptures.

04:00pm It's now time for Dante as well as a truly delicious ice cream: Go down the **Via del Proconsolo** slightly away from the crowds of tourists and take a detour **along the Via Dante Alighieri** to ⓭ **Dante's birthplace** → p. 29, before wandering through the **Borgo degli Albizi.** Anyone coming towards you devouring an ice cream has just been to ⓮ **Vivoli** → p. 66 – the city's best ice cream parlour! **Just a few steps along the Via Torta** and the Piazza Santa Croce will appear before you like a theatrical backdrop with its splendid Franciscan church ⓯ **Santa Croce** → p. 52, Florence's equivalent to the pantheon. Now dash to visit the church's leather workshop ⓰ **Scuola del Cuoio** → p. 79 before it closes at 5:30 pm where the King of Morocco and the English aristocracy are among its regular customers. It's now time for an aperitif and a snack at ⓱ **Moyo** → p. 88 close by before finishing the day in style with a performance at the historical box theatre ⓲ **Teatro della Pergola** → p. 84.

❼ Cappelle Medicee

❽ Gozzi Sergio

❾ Mercato Centrale

❿ Duomo di Santa Maria del Fiore

⓫ Baptistery

⓬ Grande Museo del Duomo

⓭ Dante's birthplace

⓮ Vivoli

⓯ Santa Croce

⓰ Scuola del Cuoio

⓱ Moyo

⓲ Teatro della Pergola

FROM SANTA MARIA NOVELLA ALONG THE SOUTHERN HEIGHTS

START: **1** Ponte Vecchio	**5 hours**
END: **1** Ponte Vecchio	Walking time (without stops) 2½ hours
Distance: **8 km/5 miles**	

COSTS: If needed, a bus ticket *biglietto 24 ore* for 5 euros
WHAT TO PACK: Comfortable shoes, camera, sun protection in summer

IMPORTANT TIPS: **4** Giardino Torrigiani: can only be visited after pre-booking, **10** Giardino dell'Iris only during these opening times: *25 April–20 May Mon–Fri 10am–1pm, 3–7.30pm, Sat/Sun 10am–7.30pm* If your feet start aching, you can always take the bus along the hillside road from Porta Romana (bus line 12).

Florence lies in a valley surrounded by hills studded with gardens belonging to the most grand ancient villas. If you enjoy a good walk, then explore the hilltops to the south of the city by foot – you'll be treated to amazing views over the city and the town of Fiesole on the opposite side of the valley.

1 Ponte Vecchio

2 Palazzo Pitti

3 Caffè Pitti

10:00am The tour starts on the "old bridge", the **1** Ponte Vecchio → p. 40, a landmark of Florence and a beautiful opportunity to view the Arno river flowing in both directions. Take the city's new pedestrian zone, **the Via Guicciardini,** to shortly arrive at the overwhelming **2** Palazzo Pitti → p. 56, once the residence of the Grand Duke of Tuscany and now home to several museums and galleries. Enjoy a cappuccino in the **3** Caffè Pitti → p. 63 opposite the palace or simply find a seat on the square to soak in the atmosphere around. After approximately 200 m/656 ft take a **right into the Via del Campuccio,** a quiet narrow street that leads you through the artisan quarters of San Frediano **straight to the Piazza Tasso.** Reserve in advance if

you want to visit the largest privately-owned gardens behind Florentine walls at the ❹ **Giardino Torrigiani** (admission 28 euros | entrance on the Via del Campuccio 55 | tel. 0 55 22 45 27 | www.giardinotorrigiani.it). From the Piazza Tasso, **follow the old city walls** until you reach the pretty ❺ **Porta Romana**.

From the Porta Romana, take the ❻ **Viale Niccolò Machiavelli** lined with trees uphill past gardens and villas to the **Piazzale Galileo** with the Hotel Kraft, also home to the Swiss Honorary Consulate. The tour then takes you along the ❼ **Viale Galileo Galilei** with its beautiful chestnut trees to the restaurant Châlet Fontana (Tue–Sun | Viale Galileo Galilei 7 | www.chaletfontana.it | Moderate), which has always been a gastronomic meeting place for the locals of Florence. But you should restrain your hunger for a little longer!

Continue along the winding road passing a viewpoint on the left overlooking the Forte di Belvedere and the hills to the east of Florence with San Domenico and Fiesole until you reach the colossal marble staircase of ❽ **San Miniato al Monte** → p. 61 on your right. Do not miss the opportunity to visit this magnificent church and its surrounding cemetery **Cimitero delle Porte Sante**, where many of the notable residents of Florence are now buried including the creator of Pinocchio, Carlo Collodi. The old

❹ Giardino Torrigiani

❺ Porta Romana

❻ Viale Niccolò Machiavelli

❼ Viale Galileo Galilei

❽ San Miniato al Monte

Adorned with riches: One jeweller after another on the Ponte Vecchio

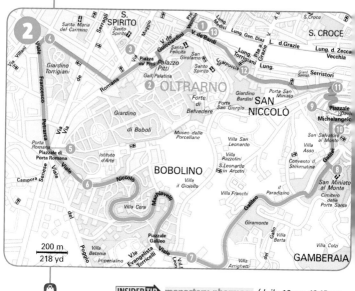

INSIDER TIP monastery pharmacy *(daily 10am–12.15pm and 4pm–6pm)* sells herbal liqueurs, candles and other souvenirs.

01:00pm Once you have left San Miniato behind you and **head down the hilltop road, you will soon reach** the vast ⑨ **Piazzale Michelangelo** → p. 61 offering stunning views across Florence literally right beneath your feet! The centre of the square is dominated by a replica of Michelangelo's David and the four allegorical sculptures of "dawn", "day", "dusk" and "night". Now it's time to take a panoramic shot of the Arno river flowing through the city and buy a tacky souvenir at one of the many stalls to remind you of your stay in Florence. If you're looking for refreshment, try the small bar with a scenic terrace located in the left-hand corner of the Piazzale. If you're visiting Florence in May, you may be lucky to catch a glimpse inside the ⑩ **Giardino dell'Iris** *(www.societaitalianairis.com)* situated below the square to the right. These gardens are only open to the public in May when visitors can view the 1,500 iris flowers in full bloom.

Now proceed down the pretty and quiet **Viale Poggi**, a long windy street with beautiful views that ends at the former city gate ⑪ **Porta San Niccolò. Take a left a**nd you'll

⑨ Piazzale Michelangelo

⑩ Giardino dell'Iris

⑪ Porta San Niccolò

soon spot the large building of the National Library on the opposite side of the river. After the next bridge, you'll come to the small ⑫ **Chiesa Evangelica Luterana** *(church service on Sundays at 10 am),* erected at the end of the 19th century for the Protestant community of Florence. The German Emperor William II was even present at its inauguration. On the opposite side of the river banks, you will now notice the arches of the Piazzale degli Uffizi as well as the enclosed passageway of the Corridoio Vasariano → p. 29 which connects the Ponte Vecchio to the Palazzo Pitti. Just a few metres further **at the Piazza Santa Maria Sopr'Arno** on the river banks is the ⑬ INSIDER TIP **Golden View Open Bar** *(daily noon–midnight | Via dei Bardi 58 | tel. 0 55 21 45 02 | www.goldenviewopenbar.com),* where you can enjoy a final drink in close proximity to your starting point at ① **Ponte Vecchio**.

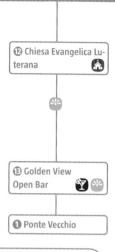

⑫ Chiesa Evangelica Luterana

⑬ Golden View Open Bar

① Ponte Vecchio

3 BY BUS TO SAN DOMENICO AND FIESOLE

START: ① Piazza San Marco **END:** ⑮ Perseus Fiesolano	1 day Walking/driving time (without stops) 1½ hours
Distance: 🔁 8.2 km/5.1 miles	

COSTS: Bus ticket *biglietto 24 ore* 5 euros, museum admission 7–17 euros
WHAT TO PACK: camera, sun protection in summer

IMPORTANT TIPS: The journey by bus to Fiesole takes just 30 minutes.

●★ Fiesole is a must-see for visitors to Florence! This small town situated at an altitude of 295 m/968 ft was founded well before Florence by the Etruscan confederacy. The well-preserved remains of the amphitheatre, Roman thermal baths and pieces of the Etruscan ancient city walls are testimony to Fiesole's glorious past.

11:00am Take the no. 7 bus at the ① **Piazza San Marco, at the corner of Via La Pira.** After a short journey through the suburbs of Florence, the route will start to ascend up a road lined with villas, gardens and olive groves. **Halfway along this road, the bus will arrive at the village of San Domenico**, a gathering of houses around the Friary of ② **San Domenico** with its church dating back to the start

① Piazza San Marco

② San Domenico

of the 15th century. Descend from the bus to take a short break here as the friary was home to the painter Fra' Angelico before he was commissioned by Cosimo de' Medici to decorate the cells of San Marco in Florence. Even today you can marvel at his large altar painting in the first chapel on the left in San Domenico as well as a crucifix in the Friary. **Opposite the church, the narrow Via di Badia** descends steeply **into the valley of Mugnone.** After just a few metres, the ❸ Badia Fiesolana *(Mon–Fri 9am–7pm),* appears on the left, an impressive Romanesque church which until 1026 was the cathedral of Fiesole. Today it is the seat of the European University Institute *(www.eui.eu).*

❸ Badia Fiesolana 🏠

Once back in the bus, **the panoramic road continues uphill leaving San Domenico behind** and the view stretches across the city to the hills of the Chianti region in the south to the highest peak of the Pratomagno mountain range in the east where snow can sometimes be spotted even in Spring. After a hairpin bend in the road, look **up the hill to your right** to see the loggia of the Villa San Michele Hotel, a former monastery which Michelangelo helped to design. **After a final bend in the road, the bus has reached the terminal at the Piazza of ❹ Fiesole.**

❹ Fiesole 🚶

12:00pm You cannot miss the overwhelming ❺ **Cattedrale di San Romolo** *(daily 7.30am–noon and 3pm–6pm, in the winter until 5pm)* built in 1028–56 and the ❻ **state seminary** located in the north-west corner of the square. With its splendid outside staircase and exotic palm trees, the ❼ **Palazzo Vescovile** (archbishops' palace) appears almost exiled into one corner of the square. **Between the seminary and the archbishops' palace, a street leads steeply upwards to the** ❽ **San Francesco monastery** *(Mon–Sat 9am–noon and 3pm–7pm, in the winter until 6pm, Sun 9am–10.30am and 3pm–7pm)* dated 1330. At a height of INSIDER TIP 345 m/1,132 ft it is the highest peak in the region and a settlement for an

❺ Cattedrale di San Romolo 🏠

❻ state seminary 🏛

❼ Palazzo Vescovile 🏛

❽ San Francesco monastery 🏠 🌳

acropolis dating back to the Etruscan and Roman periods. It is well worth the climb as on a clear day, you can enjoy a panoramic view over the entire city including the Apuan Alps mountain range!

Return to the piazza and head to ⑨ **Mastrocigliegia** *(Piazza Mino da Fiesole 3)* where truly delightful ceramics are on display! Boutiques and shops selling pretty handicrafts, food specialties and shoes are lined up on the square. **At the top of the square** you will see the ⑩ **town hall**, adorned with coats of arms and next to it the small church ⑪ **Santa Maria Primerana** (16th century) with an equestrian statue of Vittorio Emanuele II and Garibaldi standing in front. Take a break for a quick snack at ⑫ **Vinandro** *(daily noon–midnight | Piazza Mino da Fiesole 33 | tel. 05 55 91 21 | Budget–Moderate)*.

02:00pm Walk past the cathedral's apse to arrive at the ⑬ **Area Archeologica** *(Nov–Feb Wed–Mon 10am–3pm, March and Oct daily 10am–6pm, April–Sept daily 10am–7pm | admission 7 euros, joint ticket with Museo Bandini and Museo Archeologico 12 euros | www.museidifiesole.it)*, an interesting and nicely located spot to take a break in green surroundings and soak in some local culture. On this 30,000 m² archaeological site, important remains from

⑨ Mastrocigliegia

⑩ town hall

⑪ Santa Maria Primerana

⑫ Vinandro

⑬ Area Archeologica

In the Teatro Romano at Fiesole, the landscape provides a magnificent stage backdrop – just beautiful!

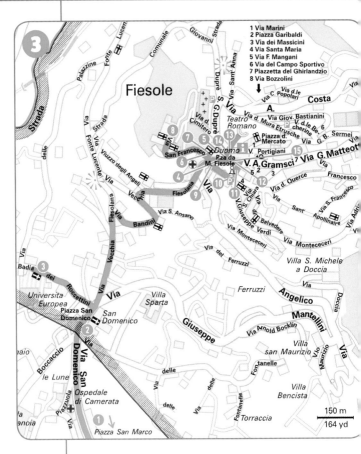

Fiesole

1 Via Marini
2 Piazza Garibaldi
3 Via dei Massicini
4 Via Santa Maria
5 Via F. Mangani
6 Via del Campo Sportivo
7 Piazzetta del Ghirlandzio
8 Via Bozzolini

150 m
164 yd

the Etruscan and Roman times have been excavated including the baths and temple. The spectacular **Teatro Romano** which once seated 3,000 people is now a popular setting for outdoor INSIDER TIP theatrical and ballet performances from the **Estate Fiesolana** → p. 114. While you are here make it also a point to see the artefacts excavated at the site on exhibition in the civic museum.

⑭ Museo Bandini 🏛

The ⑭ **Museo Bandini** *(Fri–Sun, Nov–Feb 10am–3pm, March and Oct 10am–6pm, April–Sept 9am–7pm | admission 5 euros, joint ticket with Area Archeologica and museum 12 euros | www.museidifesole.it)* **opposite the entrance to the Area Archeologica** has a small yet fine collection of works from Florentine artists from the 13th to 15th centuries. After so much sight-seeing, you have deserved a succulent *bistecca alla fiorentina* at the restaurant ⓫ **Perseus Fiesolano** *(daily | Piazza Mino da Fiesole 9 | tel. 05 55 9143 | Moderate)*. Fine Tuscan cuisine is served here in summer in the restaurant's splendid garden.

⓫ Perseus Fiesolano

4 SHOPPING IN FLORENTINE STYLE

START: ❶ Piazza della Repubblica	1/2 day
END: ⓭ Piazza Beccaria	Walking time (without stops)
Distance: ➡ 4.3 km/2.7 miles	1 hour

COSTS: Admision to Sinagoga and Museo Ebraico 6.50 euros

IMPORTANT TIPS: The ❼ **Mercato di Sant'Ambrogio** and the near-by Trippaio kiosk are both closed on Sundays

Shopping in Florence is a fantastic experience! There is something for every wallet whether you're looking for a small souvenir or exclusive brand name clothes. The shopping triangle Via Tornabuoni/Vigna Nuova/Strozzi can make you ecstatic just as much as a Milan fashion show. Yet have you ever fancied strolling down the streets off the beaten track, shopping, enjoying a *caffè* on the corner and taking in a bite to eat away from the tourist crowds just like the locals of Florence? If so, then head east away from the city centre.

11:00am From the ❶ **Piazza della Repubblica head along the lively Via del Corso** and past the small church **of** ❷ **Santa Maria de'Ricci** dating back to the early 16th century. It invites you to look inside especially if you hear sounds of classical music. Your shopping tour starts here with a selection

❶ Piazza della Repubblica

❷ Santa Maria de'Ricci

Starting point Piazza della Repubblica

Strolling along with impressive Renaissance palazzi as a backdrop: Borgo degli Albizi

of small boutiques and wine shops: In **Matucci** you'll find a tempting collection of exclusive names in fashion, **Fabriano** sells the finest stationery items while at the **Galleria del Chianti** you'll be treated to fine wines, olive oil and other delicatessens. **Lush** lures you in from the street with its smells of hand-made cosmetics.

Go straight on through the shaded passageway of Borgo degli Albizi and past the pompous Palazzo Ramirez Montalvo which houses the renowned auctioneers Pandolfini. One of the city's medieval towers, the ❸ **Torre dei Donati** dating back to the 13th century and today a Unesco world heritage site can be seen **at the Piazza San Pier Maggiore.** Pietro Annigoni (1910–88) more famously known as the "painter of he kings" once had his studio in the tower's upper floors. In the ❹ **Pizzicheria Antonio Porrati** *(Borgo degli Albizi 30r),* you can order tasty *panini* or buy a variety of delicacies. If you love ceramics, then **take a left through the low-ceiling passageway Volta di San Piero** to visit ❺ **Sbigoli Terrecotte** → p. 78. ❻ **Vestri** situated on the Piazza Salvemini is an Eldorado for chocolate lovers.

Now take the Via Pietrapiana to gradually head away from the city centre. If you've reached this point by lunch, continue just a few metres further to the old market hall of ❼ **Mercato di Sant'Ambrogio** → p. 80 on your right where you can eat in **Rocco** or head to the **kiosk of the Pollini family** on the square with the same name to try the local's favourite snack of a *panino al lampredotto* (aboma-

❸ Torre dei Donati

❹ Pizzicheria Antonio Porrati

❺ Sbigoli Terrecotte

❻ Vestri

❼ Mercato di Sant'Ambrogio

sum) or *trippa* (tripe). On your left, you'll now notice the green copper dome of the ⑧ **Sinagoga → p. 61** where you may like to step into the city's Jewish history. It is well worth a visit and is quick to reach **along the Via dei Pilastri and Via Farini. Return to the shopping mile** where you'll notice more bourgeois shoppers and far less tourists. This street lined with small shops has changed its name to **Borgo La Croce. The street ends at the vast Piazza Beccaria** with its old city gate. **Before attempting to cross this busy square,** it's worth taking a peak in the shop window of the tiny patisserie ⑨ **Dolci e Dolcezze** (Tue–Sat 8.30am–7.30pm, Sun 9am–1pm | Piazza Beccaria 8r) **on your right.**

02:00pm **Via Gioberti starts at the other end of the square,** a traditional shopping haunt of the locals. You'll literally find everything here from boutiques and jewellers to book stores, bakers, butchers, delicatessens, fishmongers or supermarkets, with bars and trattorias squeezed in between. Locals from all over Florence flock here for three different gastronomic experiences: firstly ⑩ **La Cocotte** (Mon/Tue 7.30am–8pm, Wed–Sun 7.30am–11pm | Via Gioberti 91r | www.lacocotte.org | *Moderate*), where all the ingredients used in the dishes are traditional to Tuscany. Close by is the particularly impressive assortment of wines at ⑪ **Enoteca Bonatti → p. 81.** And for first-class dairy products, cheese, ricotta, mozzarella etc. from the Mugello region, head for ⑫ **Il Palagiaccio** (Mon 4pm–7.30pm, Tue–Sat 8.30am–1pm, 4pm–7.30pm | Via Gioberti 9r | www.palagiaccio.com). **Back at the** ⑬ **Piazza Beccaria** take the trolley bus C2 to return to the city centre.

⑧ Sinagoga

⑨ Dolci e Dolcezze

⑩ La Cocotte

⑪ Enoteca Bonatti

⑫ Il Palagiaccio

⑬ Piazza Beccaria

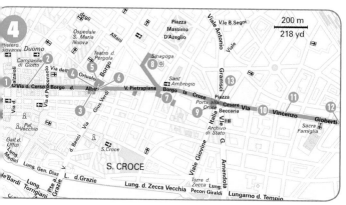

TRAVEL WITH KIDS

Very interesting for kids: The *Museo Zoologico "La Specola"* (see p. 56) has a fascinating department dedicated to anatomical models and skeletons as well as fascinating stuffed animals, from the venomous spider to the giant hippo. Or perhaps you'd find the mummies at the *Museo Archeologico* (see p. 42) more interesting?

MUSEO DI STORIA NATURALE
(134 A5) (*ᗜ G3–4*)
The Museum of Geology and Palaeontology displays over 300,000 fossils belonging to vertebrates, invertebrates and plants. Particularly impressive for children is the 4 m/13 ft high skeleton of an elephant as well as others of larger mammals. *Oct–May Mon/Tue and Thu/Fri 9.30am–4.30pm, Sat/Sun 10am–4.30pm, June–Sept Thu–Tue 10.30am–5.30pm | admission 6 euros, reduced 3 euros | Via Giorgio La Pira 4 | www.msn.unifi.it*

INSIDER TIP MUSEO STIBBERT
(133 F1–2) (*ᗜ F1*)
In 1860, Stibbert began putting together a veritable cabinet of curiosities. 64 rooms in his house are full of furniture, sculptures, costumes and other unusual objects. The heart of the collection is made up of 10,000 suits of armour and weapons from Europe, Asia and Africa. The *Sala di Cavalcata* features a parade of 14 knights and horses in full armour from the 16th century! The villa is surrounded by a spacious park – a good place for a picnic. *Park: April–Oct Fri–Wed 8am–7pm, Nov–Mar Fri–Wed 8am–5pm | free admission; Museum: all year round Mon–Wed 10am–2pm, Fri–Sun 10am–6pm | admission 8 euros, reduced 6 euros | Via Federigo Stibbert 26 | www.museostibbert.it | bus no. 4 from the main railway station*

ORTO BOTANICO (GIARDINO DEI SEMPLICI) (134 A5) (*ᗜ G3*)
The small botanical garden laid out by Cosimo de' Medici right in the heart of the city is the third-eldest in the world. The collection of various species of carnivorous plant is exciting for the kids. And note the over 200-year-old oak tree and the yew tree planted in 1720! *April–mid-Oct Mon/Tue and Thu/Fri 10am–7pm, mid-Oct–Mar Sat/Sun 10am–4pm | admission 6 euros, reduced 3 euros | Via Pier Antonio Micheli 3*

PARCO AVVENTURA VINCIGLIATA
(141 E2) (*ᗜ 0*)
The high-rope climbing park in Parco Avventura Vincigliata offers tree-top fun for

What to do with the bambini – Tips on how to keep toddlers, mini sporting aces and juvenile explorers happy in Florence

everyone provided you are taller than 90 cm! *Mid-April–May daily 10am–5pm, June–mid-Sept daily 10am–7pm, mid-Sept–mid-Oct Mon–Fri 2pm–6pm, Sat/Sun 10am–6pm, mid-Oct–Nov and Mar–mid-April Sat/Sun 10am–5pm | admission from 10 euros, depending on parcours | Via Vincigliata 21 | Fiesole | www.treexperience.it | bus SF*

PLAYGROUNDS
Unfortunately, there are very few playgrounds in the city. Simple, but functional could best describe the ones at the stadium (135 E4) *(₪ K3) (Viale Manfredo Fanti 4)*, in the *Giardino dell'Orticultura* (134 A3) *(₪ G2) (daily 8.30am until sunset | Via Vittorio Emanuele II 4)* with Italy's biggest tepidarium.

SPORTS AND EXERCISE
Milleunabici (www.bicifirenze.it) rent out bicycles (also with children's seats) on larger squares and at stations.

Two open-air swimming pools are popular in summer, particularly with younger guests: *Costoli (135 E6) (₪ K4) (June–Aug Tue, Wed, Fri 10am–6pm, Mon 2pm–6pm, Thu and Sun 10am–8pm | admission 8 euros, after 2pm 5.50 euros, children under 6 free, entry only with valid ID | Piazza Berlinguer 2 | tel. 05 56 23 60 27)* close to the stadium and the *Bellariva (141 F3) (₪ L6) (June–Aug Mon–Fri 10am–6pm, Sat/Sun 9.30am–7pm | admission 7 euros, 7–13-year-olds 5 euros | Lungarno Aldo Moro 6)*.

INSIDER TIP ▶ VILLA DEMIDOFF
(141 E2) *(₪ 0)*
Run around, have a picnic, go for a walk: all this is possible in the park of the Renaissance villa by Bernardo Buontalenti in the north of Florence. Highlight: The giant Appenin (14 m/46 ft high). *April–Oct 10am–8pm | free admission | Via Fiorentina 282 | Pratolino-Vaglia | www.provincia.fi.it/pratolino.htm | bus no. 25 from the Piazza San Marco/Via La Pira*

FESTIVALS & EVENTS

Whether it's the superb concerts during the Maggio Musicale Fiorentino, the Estate Fiesolana summer festival, the celebration of the iris or the large biennial antiques fair and the wine festivals in the autumn – there is something to suit every taste in Florence. All events under *www.italiafestival.it* or *www.fionline.it/turismo*.

FESTIVALS & EVENTS

MARCH/APRIL

25 March (Annunciation Day): Festival on the Piazza Santissima Annunziata
Taste (www.tastefirenze.it): culinary fair on a weekend in March
Scoppio del Carro on Easter Sunday: Renaissance firework, during which a historical wooden cart is set on fire between the cathedral and the baptistery
End of April: Arts and crafts fair *Mostra Internazionale dell'Artigianato (www.mostraartigianato.it)* in the Fortezza da Basso
Notte Bianca: free concerts, performances and other events in the night to 1 May

MAY/JUNE

★ *Maggio Musicale Fiorentino (tickets tel. 0 55 211158 | www.maggiofiorentino.*

com): everal weeks long festival, with operas, concerts and ballets, free closing concert on the Piazza della Signoria
Festival Fabbrica Europa (www.ffeac.org): International festival in the Stazione Leopolda with dance, music and drama
Mostra dell'Iris (www.irisfirenze.it): Huge iris show (the emblem of Florence) below the Piazzale Michelangelo
INSIDER TIP ▶ *Artigianato e Palazzo (www.artigianatoepalazzo.it)* on the 2nd or 3rd weekend in May in the garden of the Palazzo Corsini sul Prato: sale of traditional Italian crafts, also made on the premises
Calcio in Costume (www.calciostoricofiorentino.it) on June 24 in honour of the city's patron saint: football between the four districts in medieval costume on the Piazza Santa Croce; in the evening, on the Piazzale Michelangelo large ● firework display, best enjoyed from the other side of the Arno.

JULY/AUGUST

Florence Dance Festival (www.florencedance.org): Dance festival in July in the inner courtyard of the Museo del Bargello with international programme
Estate Fiesolana (www.estatefiesolana.it): One of Italy's oldest festivals, with

Naturally enough, culture plays a huge role in the Florentine calendar, but the city has a raft of other events to show for itself

concerts, ballet and films in the Roman theatre in Fiesole

SEPTEMBER/OCTOBER

INSIDER TIP **Festa della Rificolona** on 7 Sept: Innumerable paper lanterns glow on the Piazza della SS. Annunziata and the Arno.

Festival Internazionale Musica dei Popoli (www.musicadeipopoli.com) in October: Musical culture from many countries at the Auditorium Flog

Biennale Internazionale dell'Antiquariato di Firenze (www.biennaleantiquariato. it): Antiques fair at the Palazzo Corsini sull'Arno, every two years only in odd-numbered years

Festival dei Popoli (www.festivaldeipopoli.org): International documentary film festival in late October/early November

NOVEMBER/DECEMBER

Lo Schermo dell'Arte (www.schermodelarte.org): international film festival with documentaries, workshops, video installations and interesting encounters with artists from all over the world

Stagione Lirica (www.boxofficetoscana. it): High point of the concert and theatre season on almost all stages in town

NATIONAL HOLIDAYS

1 Jan	New Year's Day
6 Jan	Epiphany
March/April	Easter Sunday/ Monday
25 April	Celebration of the Liberation from Fascism
1 May	Labour Day
2 June	Republic Day
24 June	Patron Saint's Day
15 Aug	Assumption
1 Nov	All Saints' Day
8 Dec	Immaculate Conception
25/26 Dec	Christmas

LINKS, BLOGS, APPS & MORE

www.firenzeturismo.it The official city portal informs you about current events and museums, helps with the search for accommodation and offers a wide selection of maps and brochures, including city plans or wine guides to download

www.googleartproject.com/museums/uffizi/the-birth-of-venus Not even in the Uffizi can you get so close to these famous works by Giotto, da Vinci, Michelangelo, Titian or Caravaggio. And, what's more, here you can examine them at your leisure

www.luisaviaroma.com/en/diary Full of everything you need to know about the latest fashions and shows in the city. The fashion temple "Luisa Via Roma" keeps you informed with up-to-the-minute news

blog.tianakai.com Entertaining blog by a young American woman married to a Florentine guy who posts amusing anecdotes about events, everyday situations and curiosities such as fish pedicures to soothe the tired feet of tourists

www.girlinflorence.com Fabulous blog with many photos by Georgette, a Texan living in Florence. Everything about restaurants, things to do, events, getting married in Florence, shopping and much more

www.lostinflorence.it Very chic blog about the most elegant (and often slightly hidden) places to wine, dine and shop in Florence

best-of-florence.blogspot.com Florence blog with a lot of snapshots, ideas and inspirations which offers custom-made navigation and views

www.facebook.com/tfnews?ref=ts The English-language city paper, *The Florentine,* appears every two weeks; a lively Facebook community has developed from it, too

Regardless of whether you are still researching your trip or already in Florence: these addresses will provide you with more information, videos and networks to make your holiday even more enjoyable

www.vimeo.com/18268458 A little romance in your home: take a walk through Florence in the red-gold light of sunset

short.travel/flo9 Not every traveller to Florence is lucky enough to watch the *calcio storico* live so this documentary entitled "Florence Fight Club" (85 min., English subtitles) provides a lively documentation of this event and its tradition

short.travel/flo4 If your own computer is a little underpowered: Google has flown with a 3D camera over the city for Google Earth. You can look at the video in various resolutions up to HD quality

www.vimeo.com/8331012 Florence actually stands for summer, sun and warmth. In early 2011, snow brought the city to a standstill, when 30 cm of snow fell in just a few hours. There were too few snow ploughs, traffic ground to a halt and it was eerily silent. A dream of winter, captured on video

Florence Heritage How did Florence get to be a Unesco World Heritage Site? Learn it here – on twelve different city walks, for example

Firenze Card A sensible addition to the card of the same name – museums, events, Wifi hotspots – also offline

Firenze Up Florence in your pocket: events, happenings and more, filtered according to your wishes and preferences, issued by the city of Florence. Alongside the app, there's the website *eventi.comune.firenze.it*

Firenze The Walking City Nice city walks focusing on certain topics and including many sights, places of art, culture and oddities

Osterie d'Italia Are you looking for a special restaurant? The Italian Slow Food organisation recommends good places and shows you the best dishes to look forward to – mouthwatering!

TRAVEL TIPS

ARRIVAL

If you are travelling by car, take either the *Brenner highway E 45* (Brenner–Verona–Modena-Bologna), the *Gotthard highway E 35* (Lugano–Milan–Bologna) or go through Liechtenstein and the San Bernardino tunnel. Don't leave the highway until the Firenze-Certosa exit; in this way you can avoid the chaos of the suburbs and drive via the Piazzale Michelangelo (well signposted, but take care!) down into the city centre *(centro)*.

Most trains arriving from other major European cities via France, Switzerland (Basel–Milan), Germany or Austria (Munich–Brenner) stop in Florence at the main railway station, Santa Maria Novella in the centre; a few go to the through station Firenze Campo di Marte. From here, there is a suburban train to the main station. *www.trenitalia.it, www.italotreno.it*

RESPONSIBLE TRAVEL

It doesn't take a lot to be environmentally friendly whilst travelling. Don't just think about your carbon footprint whilst flying to and from your holiday destination but also about how you can protect nature and culture abroad. As a tourist it is especially important to respect nature, look out for local products, cycle instead of driving, save water and much more. If you would like to find out more about eco-tourism please visit: *www.ecotourism.org*

The *Aeroporto Amerigo Vespucci* lies just a few kilometres from the city. The airport shuttle *Vola in Bus! (daily 6am–11.30pm | fare 6 euros, return 10 euros)* takes you to the main railway station in 30 minutes. Line 2 of the *tramvia* (tram) is expected to open any day now. The taxi ride costs you between 20 and 23 euros, plus 1 euro per piece of baggage (except hand luggage). From London British Airways and Vueling fly directly to Florence, from other European countries you can fly with e.g. Air Dolomiti, Lufthansa, Swiss, Eurowings or SAS. The airport at Pisa, the *Aeroporto Galileo Galilei*, is a major North Italian hub with good international links, served by carriers like Easyjet, Ryanair or Eurowings. From here, irregular, direct trains take you to the main station in Florence *(journey time 70 mins | fare 7.80 euros)* or the *Terravision* buses *(4.99 euros | journey time 60 minutes, depending on traffic)*. Bologna airport is served by Easyjet, Eurowings, Ryanair and Vueling. You can get there in 30 minutes by fast train from the station; the fare is just under 30 euros.

BANKS

Banks are open Mon–Fri 8.20am–1.20pm and 2.45pm–3.45pm. Most branches have ATMs for use with credit cards, too.

BICYCLE, SEGWAY & VESPA

Bikesharing hit Florence in the summer of 2017: Simply download the *Mobike* app, find a bike nearest you and unlock it with the QR code. Today, these orange bikes are located all over the city and once you've used them, you can leave them

From arrival to weather

Your holiday from start to finish: useful addresses and information for your trip to Florence

wherever it's convenient for you. A 30 minute ride costs around 50 cents so far. *Florence by bike* (133 F5) (*Ⓜ F3*) *(Mon–Fri 9am–1pm and 3.30pm–7.30pm, Sat (April–Oct also Sun) 9am–7pm | Via San Zanobi 54r | tel. 05 55 48 89 92 | www.florencebybike.it)* hires out various types of two-wheeler. Price example: mountain bike: 4 euros/hr, 23 euros/day; city bike: 3 euros/hr, 14 euros/day.

Segways can be hired from *Segway Firenze* (130 C4) (*Ⓜ E5*) *(daily 10am–7pm | Via Guelfa 1h | tel. 0 55 28 56 00 | www.segwayfirenze.com)* for 19 euros/hr.

Florence has the highest number of Vespas in Italy – join the masses and drive a Vespa 125 with a companion for 60 euros/day and 150 euros/weekend from *Vesparental* (137 D1) (*Ⓜ D4*) *(April–Oct daily 9.30am–5.30pm, Nov–March closed Sun, Dec–Feb only by appointment | Via Il Prato 50r | tel. 05 53 8 50 45; mobile phone 34 97 85 25 32 | www.vesparental.eu).*

CONSULATES & EMBASSIES

UK CONSULATE
Lungarno Corsini 2 | tel. 05 52 84 133 | consular.florence@fco.gov.uk
US CONSULATE
Lungarno A. Vespucci, 38 | tel. 05 52 66 951 | uscitizensflorence@state.gov

CUSTOMS

EU citizens can import and export goods for their personal use tax-free. Visitors from other countries, including those travelling to Florence via Switzerland, must observe the following limits, except for items for personal use. Duty free are: max. 50 g perfume, 200 cigarettes, 50 cigars, 250 g

BUDGETING

Espresso	£ 0.99/$ 1.27	*for a cup of espresso at the bar*
Carriage	from £ 45/$ 57	*for a 20-minute ride*
Ice cream	from £ 1.80/$ 2.30	*for a portion with two flavours*
Snack	from £ 7.25/$ 9.25	*for lunch in a bar*
Bus ride	£ 1.09/$ 1.38	*for a ticket valid for 90 mins.*
Airport transfer	approx. £ 22/$ 29	*for a taxi into town (plus baggage)*

tobacco, 1 l of spirits (over 15 % vol.), 2 l of spirits (under 15 % vol.), 2 l of any wine.

DRIVING/CAR HIRE

Ⓥ The entire city centre is only accessible for motor vehicles with prior permission at the following times: Mon–Fri 7.30am–7.30pm and Sat until 6pm, as well as June–Sept also Thu–Sat from 11pm–3am (permits available from the *Polizia Municipale (Piazza della Calza 2* (137 D5) (*Ⓜ D6*) *| tel. 0 55 32 83 40 7 and Piazzale di Porta al Prato 6 |* (130 C5) (*Ⓜ D3*) *| tel. 05 53 28 32 84).* If you are staying in the centre (*Zona ZTL*), have your hotel issue you with a permit in advance. It is also forbidden to park in many streets in the outer districts (residents only: *divieto di sosta e parcheggio per non residenti).* Your car will be towed away and can only be retrieved upon payment of a hefty fine the following day at the out-of-town (!) *Via Allende 18/20* (137 E2) *(m 0) (tel. 05 54 22 41 42 | bus 57 and 23 from the main railway station)*. Parking spaces marked in blue are liable to charge (parking meter); white ones are for residents only!

There are 24-hour car parks at the Porta Romana/Oltrarno (136–137 C–D5) *(m D6–7)* and large underground car parks under the *Parterre* close to the Piazza della Libertà *(entrance in Via Madonna della Tosse)*; at the Fortezza da Basso (133 D4) *(m E3) (entrance in Piazzale Caduti dei Lager)* and at the Piazza Beccaria (138 C2) *(m H–J5)*. The underground car parks at the main railway station (133 D6) *(m E4) (entrance in Via Alamanni)*, at the Mercato Centrale (130 C2) *(m F4) (entrance on Via S. Antonino)* and at the Stazione Leopolda (132 C5) *(m D4)* are the most central. Prices vary between 1.50 euros/ hr and 72 euros/day. More information under: *www.firenzeparcheggi.it*

Petrol stations are located on the main arterial roads *(Mon–Fri 7:30am– 12:30pm and 3pm (3.30pm)–7:30pm)*. Self-service stations are usually open 24 hours. You have the choice of premium and diesel – and the use of methane and liquefied petroleum gas has also increased. Carsharing has also become a popular mobility option in Florence: *car-2go* for 0.26 euros/min. or 59 euros/24 h *(www.car2go.com)* and *Enjoy* for 0.25 euros/min. or 50 euros/24 h *(www.enjoy. eni.com)*. It is advisable to book your hire car before you leave home. Almost all major car-hire companies have branches in Florence, e.g. *Avis Autonoleggio* (137 D2) *(m E5) (Borgo Ognissanti 128r | tel. 0 55 21 36 29 | www.avisautonoleggio. it)*. *City Car Rent* (133 D6) *(m E4) (Via L. Alamanni 3a | tel. 05 52 39 92 31 | www. citycarrent.org)* also hires out Smarts by the hour at reasonable rates.

Emergency breakdown service (Italy-wide): Automobile Club d'Italia | *tel. 80 31 16*

BOAT TRIPS

The traditional sand diggers on the Arno have fitted out their boats to accommodate passengers, taking them for a peaceful, relaxing one-hour trip under the bridges of the city and regaling them with tales of past times and their arduous work. In the evenings in particular, when the palaces along the river banks are lit up, this is a delightful way to see Florence! From May to September – water levels permitting. Minimum 5 persons. *Per person: 12 euros | tel. info/booking through Antonio Bellacci 34 77 98 23 56 | www.renaioli.it*

EMERGENCY

Carabinieri: tel. 112; fire brigade: tel. 115; police (accident): tel. 113; emergency doctor: tel. 118

FIRENZE CARD

If you are staying for a few days, this card really is a worthwhile investment. The 72 hour card gives you free admission to 72 museums, villas and churches in the city. The major advantage: it gives you fast-lane access to museums (just show your card at the entrance to the museum). The card costs 72 euros and can be purchased at hotels, museums, or online *(www.firenzecard.it)*. The 72-hour card is valid from its first use. Each card is also valid for one child under 18-years of age.

HEALTH

CHEMIST

24-hour: *Farmacia Comunale no. 13* (130 A1) (*ⴔ E4*) at the main station; *Farmacia Molteni* (130 C4) (*ⴔ F5*) (*Via Calzaiuoli 7r*) and *Farmacia all'Insegna del Moro* (130 C3) (*ⴔ F4*) (*Piazza S. Giovanni 20r*).

HOSPITAL

Outpatient treatment around the clock at the *Pronto Soccorso* at the *Ospedale di Careggi* (141 E2) (*ⴔ 0*) and the *Ospedale Santa Maria Nuova* (131 E3) (*ⴔ G4*) (*Piazza Santa Maria Nuova 1*). For children: *Nuovo Ospedale Meyer* (141 E2) (*ⴔ 0*) (*Villa Ognissanti Viale Pieraccini 24 | Careggi | tel. 05 55 66 21*).

INFORMATION IN ADVANCE

ITALIAN STATE TOURIST BOARD

– *1 Princes Street, London W1B 2AY | tel. 020 74 08 12 54 | info.london@enit.it*
– *686 Park Avenue, New York NY 10065 | tel. 212 245-5618 | newyork@enit.it*
– *Level 2, 140 William Street, East Sydney, NSW 2011, Australia | tel. 02 9357 2561 | sydney@enit.it*

INFORMATION IN FLORENCE

Information brochures, city maps and hotel reservations at the *Infopoints: Piazza Stazione 4* (130 A2) (*ⴔ E4*) | *Mon–Sat 9am–7pm, Sun 9am–2pm | tel. 0 55 2 12 2 45; Via Cavour 1r* (130 C2) (*ⴔ F4*) | *Mon–Fri 9am–1pm | tel. 0 55 29 08 32; Aeroporto Amerigo Vespucci/arrivals hall | daily 9am–7pm | tel. 0 55 31 58 74; Piazza San Giovanni* (131 D3) (*ⴔ F5*) | *Mon–Sat 9am–7pm, Sun 9am–2pm | tel. 0 55 28 84 96.* Written enquiries to: *Via Manzoni 16 | 50121 Firenze | www.firenzeturismo.it.* The Infopoints have free publications, *Informacittà (www.informacitta.it)* and *Firenze dei Teatri (www.firenzedeiteatri.it)* which give details of events. *Firenze Spettacolo (www.firenzespettacolo.it)* has a monthly event calendar and is available from kiosks for 2 euros. Another good source of information is *The Florentine (www.theflorentine.net)*, available for free in hotels, internet points, bookshops or language schools: events, culture, food and drink as well as current news. The websites *www.firenzeturismo.it* and *www.eventi-firenze.it* have tons of information on Florence and Tuscany. Tips for shopping, sightseeing, restaurants, hotels and current exhibitions can be found at *www.visitflorence.it*. Take a virtual journey through the city with *www.italyguides.it/us/florence/florence_italy.htm*.

CURRENCY CONVERTER

£	€	€	£
1	1.15	1	0.87
3	3.45	3	2.61
5	5.74	5	4.35
13	14.93	13	11.32
40	46	40	35
75	86	75	65
120	138	120	104
250	287	250	218
500	574	500	435

$	€	€	$
1	0.88	1	1.13
3	2.64	3	3.40
5	4.41	5	5.67
13	11.46	13	14.75
40	35	40	45
75	66	75	85
120	106	120	136
250	220	250	284
500	441	500	567

For current exchange rates see www.xe.com

INTERNET & WIFI

Almost all hotels have WiFi connections. The city of Florence has by now activated 450 free hotspots. Popular Internet access points are *Internet Train* (130 C1) *(🐚 F4) (Via Guelfa 54/56r)*; *Via de' Benci 36r* (131 E5) *(🐚 G5)*; *Via Porta Rossa 38r* (130 C4) *(🐚 F5)* and *Web-puccino* (133 F5) *(🐚 F4) (daily 10am–10pm | Via dei Conti 22/r.)*

INVOICES & RECEIPTS

You can only pay cash up to an amount of 999.99 euros. According to an Italian law against tax evasion, all invoices and receipts – even the ones for a quick *caffè* in a bar – must be retained until the customer is at least 100 m (110 yd) away from the place of purchase.

PHONE & MOBILE PHONE

Since roaming charges no longer apply when you are abroad in Europe, you can now use your mobile phone for no more than you would be charged in the UK. The area code in Italy is part of the telephone number and must always be dialled (including the zero!). The international dialling code for Italy is 0039. Dial 0044 for calls from Italy to the UK; 001 to the USA; reverse-charge calls under *Tel. 8 00 17 24 90.*

There are only few phone booths (and phone cards) left. Buy a telephone card *(scheda telefonica)* at tobacconist's and kiosks; tear off the corner at the perforation before using!

POST

In all EU countries postage for standard letters and postcards is 1 euro. Stamps can be bought at the *Posta Centrale* (130 C4) *(🐚 F5) (Via Pellicceria 1)* and in many tobacconist's (look out for signs with a white "T" on a black background).

PUBLIC TRANSPORT

Transport company ATAF's tickets can be purchased in bars, tobacconist's or kiosks and must be validated on board the bus. Between 9pm and 6am, you can buy tickets for 2 euros from the bus driver. Be careful, though: The driver is not obliged to have sufficient change! Fare dodging is penalised with a fine of up to 240 euros! Children up to 1 m (3.28 ft) in height travel free. A ticket valid for 90 mins *(biglietto semplice)* costs 1.20 euros; a ticket for four journeys *(quattro corse)* 4.70 euros; a 24-hour *biglietto 24 ore* 5 euros and a 3-day ticket *(biglietto tre giorni)* 12 euros. Timetable information is available in the entrance hall of the main railway station *(daily 7.30am–7.30pm)*. The new mobile ticketing (1.50 euros plus additional SMS costs) is an uncomplicated option for anyone who uses an Italian operator (Wind, Tim, Vodafone and Tre): To access, simply send a text with the words "ATAF" to 4 88 01 05 and within a few seconds you'll receive your e-ticket (valid for 90 minutes).

Line 1 on the *tramvia* tram system takes you from the central station to the suburb of Scandicci while line 2 will open soon and will connect the university quarter in Novoli with the airport. The planned line 3 will go from Santa Maria Novella to the Careggi hospital.

SIGHTSEEING TOURS

City-Sightseeing Firenze (see p. 56) offers an easy tour (also nice for kids) with many hop on/hop off possibilities. Agencies offering individual sightseeing tours on foot or by bike for single travellers or groups must be reserved in advance, e.g. *Florence and Tuscany Tours (Via della Condotta 12 | tel. 0 55 21 03 01 | www.flo renceandtuscanytours.com | mobile tel. 34 93 16 46 77), Art Viva Walking Tours (Via dei Sassetti 1 | tel. 05 52 64 50 33 | mobile tel. 32 96 13 27 30 | www.italy. artviva.com)* and *I bike Florence (Via de'Lamberti 1 | tel. 05 52 81 103 | www. ibikeflorence.com).*

A tour with the ● *electric minibus C3* almost constitutes a city sightseeing tour. It passes along the narrow streets of the old town and takes you across to the other side of the Arno. And the journey won't break the bank *(1.20 euros).*

TAXI

In Florence it is virtually impossible to flag down a taxi. Either you call a radio taxi *(tel. 0 55 43 90; 0 55 47 98; 0 55 42 42),* or go to a taxi rank: *Main station* (130 A1–2) *(Ⓜ E4), Piazza della Libertà* (134 A4) *(ⓂG2), Piazza della Re- pubblica* (130 C3–4) *(Ⓜ F5), Piazza San Marco* (134 A5) *(Ⓜ G4), Piazza Santa Maria Novella* (130 A2–3) *(Ⓜ E4), Pi- azza Santa Trìnita* (130 B4) *(Ⓜ E5)* and *Porta Romana* (136–137 C–D5) *(Ⓜ D7).* The minimum fare at a taxi rank is 3.30 euros; if you book by phone, 5.30 euros. A supplement is charged after 10pm, on Sundays and public holidays and for each piece of baggage carried in the boot of the car. Women travelling alone at night (9pm–2am) receive a 10 per cent dis- count (ask for the *sconto*!).

THEFT

Thefts of identity cards, passports, vehi- cles, etc. must be reported to the police immediately, at a district police station or the headquarters *(Borgo Ognissanti 48 |* (137 D2) *(Ⓜ E5) | tel. 05 52 48 11).*

WEATHER IN FLORENCE

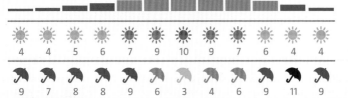

	Jan	Feb	March	April	May	June	July	Aug	Sept	Oct	Nov	Dec
Daytime temperatures in °C/°F	8/46	10/50	14/57	19/66	23/73	28/82	31/88	30/86	26/79	19/66	13/55	9/48
Nighttime temperatures in °C/°F	2/36	3/37	6/43	9/48	13/55	16/61	19/66	19/66	16/61	12/54	7/45	3/37
☀ Sunshine hours/day	4	4	5	6	7	9	10	9	7	6	4	4
☂ Precipitation days/month	9	7	8	9	6	6	3	4	6	9	11	9

☀ Sunshine hours/day   ☂ Precipitation days/month

USEFUL PHRASES ITALIAN

PRONUNCIATION

c, cc	before e or i like ch in "church", e.g. ciabatta, otherwise like k
ch, cch	like k, e.g. pacchi, che
g, gg	before e or i like j in "just", e.g. gente, otherwise like g in "get"
gl	like "lli" in "million", e.g. figlio
gn	as in "cognac", e.g. bagno
sc	before e or i like sh, e.g. uscita
sch	like sk in "skill", e.g. Ischia
z	at the beginning of a word like dz in "adze", otherwise like ts

An accent on an Italian word shows that the stress is on the last syllable. In other cases we have shown which syllable is stressed by placing a dot below the relevant vowel.

IN BRIEF

Yes/No/Maybe	Sì/No/Forse
Please/Thank you	Per favore/Grazie
Excuse me, please!	Scusa!/Mi scusi
May I...?/Pardon?	Posso...? / Come dice?/Prego?
I would like to.../Have you got...?	Vorrei.../Avete...?
How much is...?	Quanto costa...?
I (don't) like that	(Non) mi piace
good/bad	buono/cattivo/bene/male
broken/doesn't work	guasto/non funziona
too much/much/little/all/nothing	troppo/molto/poco/ tutto/niente
Help!/Attention!/Caution!	aiuto!/attenzione!/prudenza!
ambulance/police/fire brigade	ambulanza/polizia/vigili del fuoco
Prohibition/forbidden/danger/dangerous	divieto/vietato/pericolo/pericoloso
May I take a photo here/of you?	Posso fotografar La?

GREETINGS, FAREWELL

Good morning!/afternoon!/ evening!/night!	Buon giorno!/Buon giorno!/ Buona sera!/Buona notte!
Hello! / Goodbye!/See you	Ciao!/Salve! / Arrivederci!/Ciao!
My name is...	Mi chiamo...
What's your name?	Come si chiama?/Come ti chiami
I'm from...	Vengo da...

Parli italiano?

"Do you speak Italian?" This guide will help you to say the basic words and phrases in Italian.

DATE & TIME

Monday/Tuesday/Wednesday	lunedì/martedì/mercoledì
Thursday/Friday/Saturday	giovedì/venerdì/sabato
Sunday/holiday/	domenica/(giorno) festivo/
working day	(giorno) feriale
today/tomorrow/yesterday	oggi/domani/ieri
hour/minute	ora/minuto
day/night/week/month/year	giorno/notte/settimana/mese/anno
What time is it?	Che ora è? Che ore sono?
It's three o'clock/It's half past three	Sono le tre/Sono le tre e mezza
a quarter to four	le quattro meno un quarto/
	un quarto alle quattro

TRAVEL

open/closed	aperto/chiuso
entrance/exit	entrata/uscita
departure/arrival	partenza/arrivo
toilets/ladies/gentlemen	bagno/toilette/signore/signori
(no) drinking water	acqua (non) potabile
Where is...?/Where are...?	Dov'è...?/Dove sono...?
left/right/straight ahead/back	sinistra/destra/dritto/indietro
close/far	vicino/lontano
bus/tram	bus/tram
taxi/cab	taxi/tassì
bus stop/cab stand	fermata/posteggio taxi
parking lot/parking garage	parcheggio/parcheggio coperto
street map/map	pianta/mappa
train station/harbour	stazione/porto
airport	aeroporto
schedule/ticket	orario/biglietto
supplement	supplemento
single/return	solo andata/andata e ritorno
train/track	treno/binario
platform	banchina/binario
I would like to rent...	Vorrei noleggiare...
a car/a bicycle	una macchina/una bicicletta
a boat	una barca
petrol/gas station	distributore/stazione di servizio
petrol/gas / diesel	benzina/diesel/gasolio
breakdown/repair shop	guasto/officina

FOOD & DRINK

Could you please book a table for tonight for four?	Vorrei prenotare per stasera un tavolo per quattro?
on the terrace/by the window	sulla terrazza/ vicino alla finestra
The menu, please/	La carta/il menù, per favore
Could I please have...?	Potrei avere...?
bottle/carafe/glass	bottiglia/caraffa/bicchiere
knife/fork/spoon/salt/pepper	coltello/forchetta/cucchiaio/sale/pepe
sugar/vinegar/oil/milk/cream/lemon	zucchero/aceto/olio/latte/panna/limone
cold/too salty/not cooked	freddo/troppo salato/non cotto
with/without ice/sparkling	con/senza ghiaccio/gas
vegetarian/allergy	vegetariano/vegetariana/allergia
May I have the bill, please?	Vorrei pagare/Il conto, per favore
bill/tip	conto/mancia

SHOPPING

Where can I find...?	Dove posso trovare...?
I'd like.../I'm looking for...	Vorrei.../Cerco...
Do you put photos onto CD?	Vorrei masterizzare delle foto su CD?
pharmacy/shopping centre/kiosk	farmacia/centro commerciale/edicola
department store/supermarket	grandemagazzino/supermercato
baker/market/grocery	forno/ mercato/negozio alimentare
photographic items/newspaper shop/	articoli per foto/giornalaio
100 grammes/1 kilo	un etto/un chilo
expensive/cheap/price/more/less	caro/economico/prezzo/di più/di meno
organically grown	di agricoltura biologica

ACCOMMODATION

I have booked a room	Ho prenotato una camera
Do you have any... left?	Avete ancora...
single room/double room	una (camera) singola/doppia
breakfast/half board/	prima colazione/mezza pensione/
full board (American plan)	pensione completa
at the front/seafront/lakefront	con vista/con vista sul mare/lago
shower/sit-down bath/balcony/terrace	doccia/bagno/balcone/terrazza
key/room card	chiave/scheda magnetica
luggage/suitcase/bag	bagaglio/valigia/borsa

BANKS, MONEY & CREDIT CARDS

bank/ATM/pin code	banca/bancomat/ codice segreto
cash/credit card	in contanti/carta di credito
bill/coin/change	banconota/moneta/il resto

HEALTH

doctor/dentist/paediatrician	medico/dentista/pediatra
hospital/emergency clinic	ospedale/pronto soccorso/guardia medica
fever/pain/inflamed/injured	febbre/dolori/infiammato/ferito
diarrhoea/nausea/sunburn	diarrea/nausea/scottatura solare
plaster/bandage/ointment/cream	cerotto/fasciatura/pomata/crema
pain reliever/tablet/suppository	antidolorifico/compressa/supposta

POST, TELECOMMUNICATIONS & MEDIA

stamp/letter/postcard	francobollo/lettera/cartolina
I need a landline phone card/ I'm looking for a prepaid card for my mobile	Mi serve una scheda telefonica per la rete fissa/Cerco una scheda prepagata per il mio cellulare
Where can I find internet access?	Dove trovo un accesso internet?
dial/connection/engaged	comporre/linea/occupato
socket/adapter/charger	presa/riduttore/caricabatterie
computer/battery/rechargeable battery	computer/batteria/accumulatore
internet address (URL)/e-mail address	indirizzo internet/indirizzo email
internet connection/wifi	collegamento internet/wi-fi
e-mail/file/print	email/file/stampare

LEISURE, SPORTS & BEACH

beach/bathing beach	spiaggia/bagno/stabilimento balneare
sunshade/lounger/cable car/chair lift	ombrellone/sdraio/funivia/seggiovia
(rescue) hut/avalanche	rifugio/valanga

NUMBERS

0	zero	15	quindici
1	uno	16	sedici
2	due	17	diciassette
3	tre	18	diciotto
4	quattro	19	diciannove
5	cinque	20	venti
6	sei	21	ventuno
7	sette	50	cinquanta
8	otto	100	cento
9	nove	200	duecento
10	dieci	1000	mille
11	undici	2000	duemila
12	dodici	10000	diecimila
13	tredici	½	un mezzo
14	quattordici	¼	un quarto

STREET ATLAS

The green line indicates the Discovery Tour "Florence at a glance"
The blue line indicates the other Discovery Tours
All tours are also marked on the pull-out map

Photo: Evening at the Ponte Vecchio

Exploring Florence

The map on the back cover shows how the area has been sub-divided

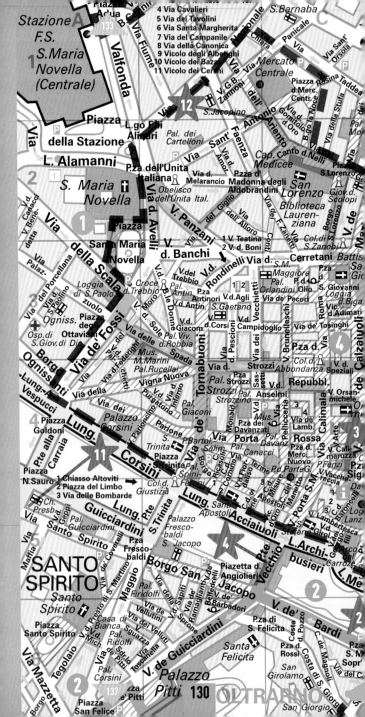

D

San Marco
Gen. M. Fanti

Cavour

3 Ricasoli

Acc. di Belle Arti
Gall dell' Accademia

Opif. d. Pietre Dure

Pal. Grifoni

E

Università

C. Battisti

Santissima Annunziata

Pza d. Ss. Annunziata

Ferdinando I

Giuseppe

Giusti

Museo Archeologico

Capponi

Gherar

N GIOVANNI

Palazzo Gerini

Panciatichi

Pal. Niccolini

Pal. Pucci

Servi

P.zz F.Brunelleschi

Mus. L. da Vinci

Retonda di S.Maria d. Agnoli

Pergola della

Laura

1

2

S. Maria Madd. de' Pazzi

Crocifission del Perugin

Via del Pucci

Via del

Piazza F. Brunelleschi

degli

Alfani

1

San Michele Visdomini

Ospedale Santa Maria Nuova

S.M. Nuova

V. Nuova de' Caccini

Vc. d. Pergola

Borgo

Pinti

Duomo

nile to

Duomo

Mus. d.Opera d.Duomo

S. Egidio

Bibl. delle Oblate

Teatro d. Pergola

Fiesolana

1

Mus. Storico Topografico

V. S.

Egidio

CENTRO

Pepi de'

Pal. Salviati

Corso

Mus. d'Antrop. e d'Etnol.

Pal. Altoviti

Teatro Oriolo

Volta di S. Piero

Piazza G. Salvemini

V. Pietrapiana

Piazza dei Ci

4

Via Bonizz

Pal.

Borgo

degli

Albizi

Pal. Quaratesi

Palazzo Alessandri

V. M. Palmieri

V. d. Badesse

Verdi

Pepi

V.d. Martini d.Pop.

del Ulivo

Log.d.Pesc

Alighieri

Badia

Via Fiorentina

Bargello

Via

Pal. dei Borghese

Ghibellina

Pandol-fini

Pal. S. Niccolo Quaratesi

Via

Rosa

Casa Buonarroti

4

Piazza di San Firenze

Via dell'

Vecchia

Teatro G.Verdi

Via Giovanni

Via d.

Fico

V.M. Buonarroti

Allegri

San Firenze

Borgo dei

Via

V. Bor gognona

V. Stinche

V. d. Lavatoi

Torta

V. d. Verrazzano

Via delle Pinzochere

V. S. Cristofano

Borgo

13

Pal. Gondi

V.d. Corno

Anguillara

P

Piazza Santa Croce

Dante

L.go P Bargellini Via di S. Giuseppe

Via dei C

5

Greci

P.zz Peruzzi

Casa d. Peruzzi

Casa d. Antella

Santa Croce

Cappella de'Pazzi

Via delle

Log.d. Grano

Borgo S.Croce

Pal. Corsini

Pal. Rasponi

Vinegia

Castello d'Altafronte

Pal. Vita

Pal. dei Mosca

Diacceto

V. d. Vagellai P.Bardi

Mus. Horne

Corso d.

Biblioteca Nazionale

Via S

6

Piazza Mentana Malenchini

Sercelli

Mozza

Tintori

Piazza dei Cavalleggeri

Via

6

 L. Gen. Diaz

sso degli Armagnati
a de' Salterelli
sso del Buco

Lungarno d. Grazie

C

Torrigiani

Lung.

Ponte a. Grazie

Fiume

Arno

Lung. Serristori

200 m
219 yd

131

138

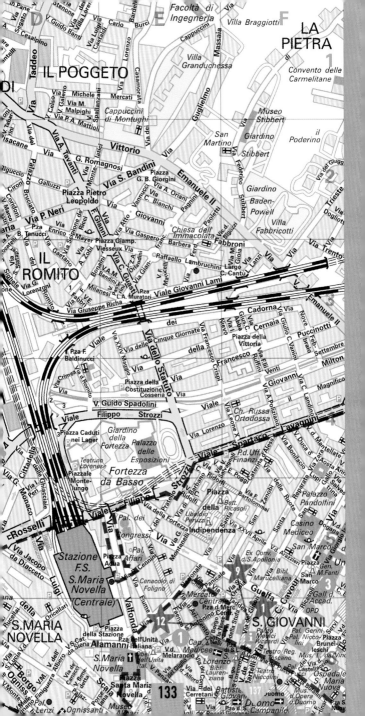

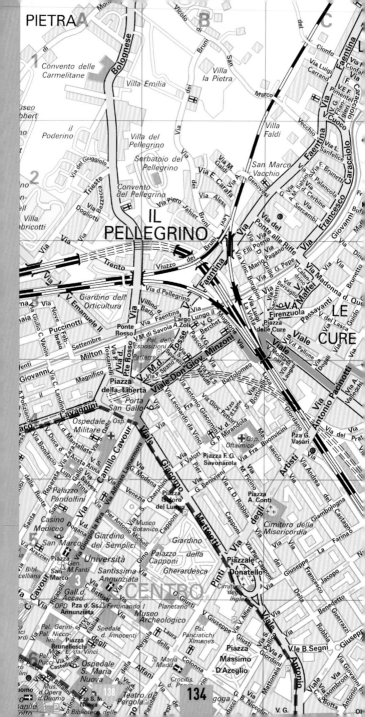

CAMERATA

IL GAROFANO

SAN GERVASIO

CAMPO DI MARTE

FILAROCCA

Fiesole

14

200 m
219 yd

Istituto Silvio Dessì

Villa Palmieri

Villa Bosco Bello

le Terrazze

Villa S. Luigi

Villa Magnolia

il Ciliegio

Villa Maria Assunta

C.R.I. Preventorio A. Torrigiani

Villa Chiari

Villa Camerata (Ostello della Gioventù)

la Squadra

Villa Baldi

Villa Pestellini

Collegio alla Querce

Villa Rasponi

la Favorita

Villa Piazza

Nuovo Gondi

Piazza T.A. Edison

Istituto Naz. dei Ciechi

Pza Ss. Gervasio e Protasio

Piazza L. Nobili

Piazza Antonelli

V. Fardella di Torrearsa

Scuola Nazionale di Pallavolo

Stadio Artemio Franchi

Campo di baseball

Stadio Luigi Ridolfi

Campo Sportivo ex Padovani

Campi di Tennis

Palazzetto dello Sport

Centro C.O.N.I.

Nelson Mandela Forum

Piscina Costoli

Largo A. Gennarelli

V-Eleon. Duse

135

Piazza
T. Jefferson
Piazzale
Catena

Teatro
Comunale
Esteristero

Piazza
Vittoria
Firenze
Porta al
prato

Viale del Visarno
Tennis
Club
Pisc.
Club
Olmi
Vittoria
Pisc. Emanuele II

Viale degli
Abramo
Lincoln

Viale Stendhal
Via delle Pietre

Viale dei Fratelli

Torre
della Serpe

Via
Solferino

Via
Scuole
Via B. di
Giovanni

Via
Giovanni da Montorsoli

del Pignone
Giov. da
tortsoli

Via
Diavoli,

Via d. Pignone
Via Jac.
Francavilla
P. Uccello

Piazza
Vittorio Veneto
Corso

Lungarno
Lungarno del Pignone
Via del Pignone

Fiorentino
Via del
Pignoncino

Via dei
Bacio Bandinelli
Via G.
Pieralla
Vittoria

Piazza
T. Gaddi

Stazione
S. Rosa
Lung.

PIGNONE
Via Jac.
Francavilla
Vignali
A. Caro

Bronzino
Via G.
d'Casa

Via Giov. A. Sogliani
Piazza
S. Maria
del Pignone
Via d. Fonderia

Fiume

Via Fra.
Filippo
Lippi
Via del Chiesino
Via L.
Maitani
Pisana
V.G.
Sospeso

Via F.
Cavallotti

Via dell'
Anconella

MONTICELLI
Villa
Strozzi
Monte Uliveto
Piazza
Pier Vettori
Via
Uliveto
Pisana

Pza di
Verzp
Porta
S.Frediano

Il Boschetto
Via
Villa
Monte Uliveto
di
Monte
Viale
R. Sanzio
Via
B. Gozzoli
Via G.
Zanella

Largo del
Boschetto

V.le Aleardo Aleardi
Via F. Berni

SA
FRE

Via Alessio
Baldovinetti
Via di San Vito
Pietro
Cosimo
Via di
Monte
Uliveto
San
Vito
Villa
Fioravanti
Via Domenico Burchiello
Via Luigi
Ariosto

Villa
Chiocchini
San
Via
Via San Francesco di Paola
Villani

Tana
Villa dello
Strozzino
Villa
Laetizia
Piazza
S.Francesco
di Paola
Via Giano Della Bella

Via
Mir

OLIVUZZO
Villa
Brichieri-Colombi
Villa Mercede
Piazza di
Bellosguardo
Via di Bellosguardo
Via
San Francesco
La Limonaia
Via
del Michelo
Via del Casor

Villa Papini
San
Carlo
Piana
Villa'
Ombrellino
Torre di Bellosguardo
Via
Ippolito Pindemonte
Via
V. Mc

Villa
Bigazzi
Torre di
Montano
BIGAZZI
BELLOSGUARDO

Villa Maria

Villa
Venturini
Convento
di Santa
Verdiana
Ugo
Via Ugo Foscolo
Foscolo
Via
Giovanni
Pietro
Metas
Prati

Maria
a
VISIBELLI
Marignolle
Villa
Rangoni
la
Colombaia
Campo

Santa
MERLI
Via
delle
Via
Campora
Sant'Ilario
a Colombaia
Via
S. Ilario
a Colombaia

Villa Fossi

le Càmpora

Via P. Mascagni
Via Cardinal Leopoldo
Via Maria Madd.
Via Pezzi
Via S. Rita da Cascia
SAN
GAGGIO
Via S.
Via Be

200 m
219 yd

136

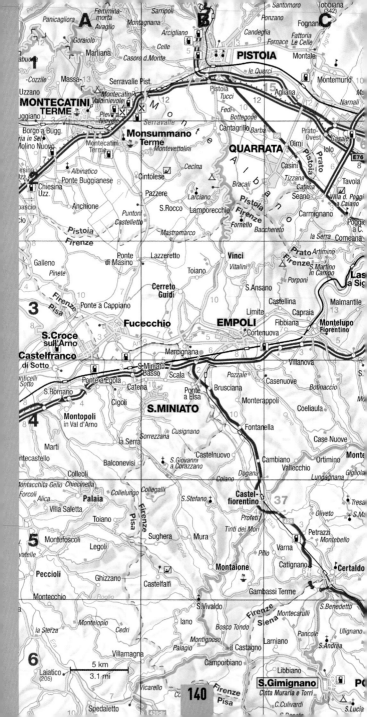

This index lists a selection of the streets and squares shown in the street atlas

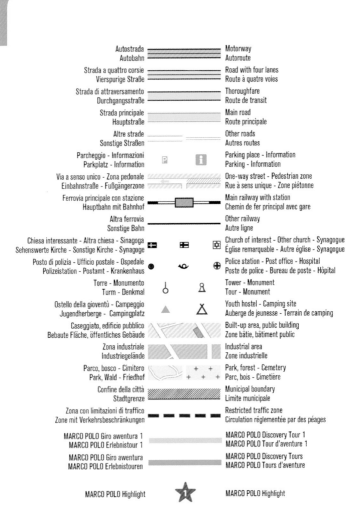

Autostrada / Autobahn	Motorway / Autoroute
Strada a quattro corsie / Vierspurige Straße	Road with four lanes / Route à quatre voies
Strada di attraversamento / Durchgangsstraße	Thoroughfare / Route de transit
Strada principale / Hauptstraße	Main road / Route principale
Altre strade / Sonstige Straßen	Other roads / Autres routes
Parcheggio - Informazioni / Parkplatz - Information	Parking place - Information / Parking - Information
Via a senso unico - Zona pedonale / Einbahnstraße - Fußgängerzone	One-way street - Pedestrian zone / Rue à sens unique - Zone piétonne
Ferrovia principale con stazione / Hauptbahn mit Bahnhof	Main railway with station / Chemin de fer principal avec gare
Altra ferrovia / Sonstige Bahn	Other railway / Autre ligne
Chiesa interessante - Altra chiesa - Sinagoga / Sehenswerte Kirche - Sonstige Kirche - Synagoge	Church of interest - Other church - Synagogue / Église remarquable - Autre église - Synagogue
Posto di polizia - Ufficio postale - Ospedale / Polizeistation - Postamt - Krankenhaus	Police station - Post office - Hospital / Poste de police - Bureau de poste - Hôpital
Torre - Monumento / Turm - Denkmal	Tower - Monument / Tour - Monument
Ostello della gioventù - Campeggio / Jugendherberge - Campingplatz	Youth hostel - Camping site / Auberge de jeunesse - Terrain de camping
Caseggiato, edificio pubblico / Bebaute Fläche, öffentliches Gebäude	Built-up area, public building / Zone bâtie, bâtiment public
Zona industriale / Industriegelände	Industrial area / Zone industrielle
Parco, bosco - Cimitero / Park, Wald - Friedhof	Park, forest - Cemetery / Parc, bois - Cimetière
Confine della città / Stadtgrenze	Municipal boundary / Limite municipale
Zona con limitazioni di traffico / Zone mit Verkehrsbeschränkungen	Restricted traffic zone / Circulation réglementée par des péages
MARCO POLO Giro awentura 1 / MARCO POLO Erlebnistour 1	MARCO POLO Discovery Tour 1 / MARCO POLO Tour d'aventure 1
MARCO POLO Giro awentura / MARCO POLO Erlebnistouren	MARCO POLO Discovery Tours / MARCO POLO Tours d'aventure
MARCO POLO Highlight	MARCO POLO Highlight

MARCO POLO TRAVEL GUIDES

INDEX

This index lists all sights, destinations and names plus a number of important streets and squares featured in this guide. Numbers in bold indicate a main entry.